THE RELUCTANT HEALER

The Reluctant Healer:

One Woman's Journey of Faith

BY EMILY GARDINER NEAL

Compiled and edited by Anne Cassel

SHAW

COLORADO SPRINGS, COLORADO

North Wind Books brings to the reader a series of biographies, imaginative literature, and popular theology designed to encourage people to follow God's call to purposeful and holy living.

The Reluctant Healer
A SHAW BOOK PUBLISHED BY WATERBROOK PRESS
5446 North Academy Blvd., Suite 200
Colorado Springs, CO 80918
A division of Random House, Inc.

The primary source for Scripture quotations in this book is the *King James Version* of the
Bible. Other sources, which Emily Gardiner Neal used, include *The Revised Standard
Version* of the Bible (copyright 1946, 1952, 1971 by the Division of Christian Education
of the National Council of the Churches of Christ in the USA, and used by permission),
The Jerusalem Bible (copyright 1966 by Darton, Longman & Todd, Ltd. and Doubleday, a
division of Bantam Doubleday Dell Publishing Group, Inc. Reprinted by permission),
The New English Bible (© The Delegates of Oxford University Press and The Syndics of
the Cambridge University Press, 1961. Reprinted with permission), and her own para-
phrasing.

ISBN 0-87788-706-3

Cover design by Justin Ahrens
Interior design by Carol Barnstable

Library of Congress Cataloging-in-Publication Data

Neal, Emily Gardiner.
      The reluctant healer / Emily Gardiner Neal.
         p. cm.
      Includes index.
      ISBN 0-87788-706-3 (pbk.)
         1. Neal, Emily Gardiner. 2. Christian Biography—United States.
      3. Healers—United States—Biography. I. Title.

BR1716.N43 A3 2000
234'.131'092—dc21
[B]
                                                              00-021176

06   05   04   03   02   01   00
10 9 8 7 6 5 4 3 2 1

Contents

Editor's Preface

———◆———

Was she reluctant? Oh, yes! As a professional reporter and writer for national publications, Emily Gardiner Neal was a woman respected for her objectivity. No wonder, then, that she wanted to withdraw from the puzzling things she began to see as she was exposed to services of Christian healing. The very premise of such healing seemed untenable or, at least, suspect. How was she to maintain her intellectual integrity in the face of her growing perception that some unknown spiritual force was at work in this world, transforming human bodies, minds, and hearts? With a good reporter's sense of fairness, though, she did investigate. And so her adventures began.

About her intellect she need not have worried. Later she was to find herself conversing as an equal with bishops, seminary deans, and other respected theologians. With these people and many other clergy she served as fellow lecturer and as minister behind the altar rail. And with them she formed many lifelong friendships.

Was she a healer? As Emily's story unfolds, each reader can decide. This book tells of many healings that occurred during her ministry over a period of four decades. Some were manifest as the instantaneous healing or alleviation of physical ills. More often, such healings were gradual. Some involved mental or emotional problems, or the restoring of relationships. Also, Emily encountered that holy mystery in which true healing is experienced in the time that precedes a patient's death. Emily teaches that God's healing power can transform *any* form of human brokenness.

We know that Emily resisted the label *healer*, because she saw herself simply as an instrument that is used for *God's* healing purposes. And she saw that the word *healer* is used to refer to many types of people—even some who might question the very existence of God. She believed that God acts unceasingly and creatively in many ways to touch human lives with healing grace. It can come through medical treatment or psychological counseling or lifestyle changes. Healing can come through the casual remark of a friend or a single riveting sentence in a borrowed book or a moving event on the television screen. Certainly, too, it can come through the church's ministry and a direct spiritual encounter with God's will for wholeness.

Seeing her role as that of an enabler for healing, Emily could write, "The healing power comes through my right hand," with no claim whatsoever that she was herself the source of that power.

The alert reader will find this idea expressed repeatedly in Emily's writings. Consider the very titles of her books: *God Can Heal You Now* and *The Healing Power of Christ*. She never wavered in her desire to give God the total credit.

This selection from the writings of Emily Gardiner Neal is based on her seven books about the church's ministry of healing. The order is chronological because the sequence in which she wrote her books was determined by some of the major events in her own life—religious conversion, a new career as a healing missioner, the death of her husband, a severe physical injury, the move to a religious community. In her accounts of these events, she tells her own story and at the same time explores deeply some basic aspects of Christian healing ministry.

We began planning this project before her death in 1989 and agreed on several guidelines: to correct obvious errors of style and typography in the original books, to update the originals by eliminating dated material, to provide transitional commentary, and to retain the biblical citations. We also wished to accommodate the changes in style, outlook, and understanding that had occurred in the church over the decades since her first book. This has led to more open patterns of capitalization, punctuation, and phrasing than in the original books. Where decisions about such matters were difficult, it helped to remember that as a reporter Emily knew the importance of writing and speaking in the idiom of the day. She also saw and accepted the obvious need to abridge her original works substantially, but I hope this book retains the clarity and flow that she worked so hard to achieve.

Each of the seven main sections represents one book, with related excerpts from her other books included where it seems appropriate. Sources of these additional excerpts are identified as follows: (R) for *A Reporter Finds God*, (N) for *God Can Heal You Now*, (H) for *The Lord Is Our Healer*, (M) for *In the Midst of Life*, (S) for *Where There's Smoke*, (P) for *The Healing Power of Christ*, and (T) for *The Healing Ministry*. With each excerpt, a number designates the original page on which the quoted material begins.

Emily Gardiner Neal was not an informal person by nature, yet something about her encouraged those who knew and worked with her to use her Christian name, and that was the custom. That is why throughout this book she is referred to simply as "Emily."

She would delight in the enormous changes that are occurring today in our understanding of health and wholeness. Physicians are teaching the value of intercession; well-documented studies show the efficacy of prayer; prestigious medical schools now include in their curricula the spiritual aspects of patients' lives; clergy and medical caregivers are finding ways to collaborate. In this respect, Emily's work was prophetic. As related in chapter 5 of this book, Emily not only proclaimed what *ought* to be, she lived it out, as shown in her relationships with medical professionals. She envisioned a form of mutual ministry that would cut through our artificial boundaries between body and mind and make room for the human spirit.

Most of all, Emily hoped that each person she reached might learn to seek God for God alone: not for physical healing or emotional comfort or spiritual gifts; not for an increase in energy or relief from stress or freedom from guilt. All of these things are good, and we long for them, and they may, in fact, come to us. But the blessing to be sought, she believed, is connection with the reality that sustains the universe—the loving heart of God.

—Anne Cassel

CHAPTER ONE

A Reporter Finds God

------◆------

A Reporter Finds God Through Spiritual Healing *was
Emily Gardiner Neal's first book on the healing ministry
of the church. Published in 1956, it went through fifteen
printings and became an international landmark in the
healing ministry. Emily joined a handful of others who
were pioneers in reviving this ancient ministry that had
declined through the centuries, though it was never entirely lost to the church.*

*In the following chapters, Emily tells of beginning her
spiritual journey, which culminated many years later in
her ordination as a deacon. At the start of this adven-
ture, she was a professional writer, having begun as a
news journalist during World War II. She then turned to
freelance feature writing for national magazines. Some
fifty of her articles on a variety of topics appeared in
such periodicals as* Look, Redbook, McCall's, Reader's
Digest, *and* Woman's Day. *Thus she was well equipped
by talent and by training to tell her own unusual story.*

------◆------

First Encounter

It all began with a telephone call on a cold February
night. "The car battery's dead; they can't send a taxi for

an hour, and I'm due at an important meeting at 8 P.M.," came my new neighbor's harried voice over the wire. "Could you possibly run me over? It won't take over twenty minutes, and I'll get a taxi back."

I rather reluctantly acquiesced. After all, I scarcely knew the man. I was busy trying to meet a deadline, and the roads were a glare of ice. He joined me as I got to the car. "Say, it's nice of you to do this for me," he said. "My little girl's sick in the hospital with meningitis. Our minister was there this afternoon and laid on hands. She improved right afterwards, but the doctor said it was just temporary. He said there wasn't much hope. My wife's at the hospital now. I just felt certain that if I went to the healing service tonight and prayed for her, she'd be all right. As a sign of active faith, I wanted to get to the church myself."

I stopped short in my mental tracks. What sort of gibberish was this? Who *were* these odd people who were now my next-door neighbors?

"What church do you want to go to?" I asked as I started the engine, half hoping it wouldn't turn over. When he mentioned the local Episcopal church, I was surprised. I'd always thought of Episcopalians as ultradignified, super-conservative people. What were they doing holding "healing" services?

By the time we drew up to the church, it had started to snow. I knew in this weather it would be impossible to get a cab after the service, so I volunteered to wait and drop the man off at the hospital on the way home. The problem now was what to do with myself while he was in church. I finally accepted, with rather poor grace, I'm afraid, my companion's suggestion that I accompany him to the service.

We slipped into the first pew we came to that had two empty seats. I glanced at the woman on my left as I sat down, noticing that she seemed to have a large goiter. Something about her looked vaguely familiar.

The service opened with a hymn and a brief prayer. Then there was a short talk on spiritual healing by the priest. He pointed out that if you believed that Christ's commission to the church was to preach the kingdom of God, you must also believe that his commission was to heal, for the two commands were inseparable.

The clergyman's basic premise was that the healing power of Christ is as evident today as it was nearly two thousand years ago. He emphasized the fact that Jesus is the same, yesterday, today, and forever—and so are his works. He spoke of the power of the redemptive love of Christ, which is the healing power, and which is available to all who seek it through faith and repentance.

Obviously this was no place for me. I couldn't even accept the facts upon which the priest's basic premise had been predicated. I believed in some nebulous sort of Creator; I believed that Jesus was a great ethical and moral leader. I was far from sure that he was the Son of God, and I had never pretended to believe in the so-called miracles of his earthly ministry. I gave the clergyman credit for sincerity, thought the congregation overzealous, and closed my eyes.

Next thing I knew, I heard the clergyman summon those who sought healing, either for their souls or bodies, themselves or others, to the altar rail, for the laying-on of hands and Holy Communion.

I watched as one by one the congregation filed quietly to the altar, noticing particularly one small, redheaded boy who passed close by me, his hands a mass of warts. I watched the believers kneeling at the altar, and almost against my will I began to stop feeling supercilious.

The atmosphere was strangely charged with what seemed an almost palpable faith. An air of expectancy began to flood the dimly lit church. I listened to the priest as he laid his hands upon the head of each supplicant, intoning: "I lay my hand upon thee in the Name of the Father, and of the Son, and of the Holy Ghost."

In this company of the faithful, I felt myself an undesirable alien. I felt my presence at this service to be a sort of sacrilege. For the first time in many years, I found myself praying—to whom, I wasn't sure. "If there is a God, don't let these people down," I pleaded. "Please don't let them down, but honor their faith." It was not until some months later that I realized the absurd incongruity of an unbeliever praying to a God she didn't think existed for the benefit of this large group of men and women who knew more of faith than I could ever learn.

One by one those at the altar returned to their pews. They walked back, heads high, in quiet dignity and full confidence. As the small boy with the warts brushed by me, I looked at his hands, but he passed too quickly for me to see them. I flinched from the burning heat of his body. The thought flashed through my mind that he shouldn't be here with a temperature of at least 103.

The woman sitting beside me dropped to her knees in prayer. Although we were not touching, it seemed as if I could feel an excessive and tremendous heat emanating from her body. I thought briefly that the health authorities should step in and stop these fevered individuals from exposing others to their obviously acute infections. I glanced surreptitiously at her throat—and my heart began to pound. I could see no evidence of the swelling I had been so sure was there a short while before.

My friend rejoined me, his eyes wet, but shining with a look of such bare joy that I looked down in embarrassment—and no little apprehension. What would he do if his little girl had died while we were in church? The congregation knelt again for the blessing, and the service was over.

In walking out of the church, I looked curiously and closely at the woman who had been sitting next to me. There was no doubt of it; her neck was completely normal. *My imagination is certainly getting the better of me*, I thought. *There was probably nothing wrong with her in the first place.*

The small boy was ahead of me, now holding his father's arm. I looked at his exposed hand. I blinked and looked again. It was brown, and smooth as silk. No sign of a wart anywhere. I had the distinctly uncanny feeling that either all this was a dream, or I was losing my mind.

I left my friend off at the hospital as arranged, and went on home. I tried to finish my work, but I was too excited and puzzled by what I had seen—or did I just think I had seen it? Had I imagined the little boy's warts? No—I was sure not—but I had read somewhere of psychosomatic cures for this condition. The fact that these warts chose to disappear in the middle of a "healing" service was purely coincidental.

The swelling I thought I had observed in the neck of

the woman next to me might well have been imagined. The light was dim, and she wore a fur collar that might well have cast a shadow on her throat. And as for my neighbor's child, I only hoped she would be all right. Of course, if she were, that too was undoubtedly coincidence. Patients frequently take a sudden and unanticipated turn for the better.

About midnight I decided to call my neighbor. He answered the phone at once, and I knew by his voice that all was well. "Say, I want to thank you again for taking me—" he began. I cut him short. "What about the child?" I asked.

"She's just fine," he replied. "They can't understand at the hospital what happened—that is, nobody but our doctor can. Funny thing, but he doesn't seem surprised."

No wonder, I thought. He probably knew she had a fifty-fifty chance. She just passed some sort of crisis in her illness, that's all. Why was my heart beating faster than usual?

In the cold, clear light of the next morning, I marveled at my excitement of the night before. The whole thing now seemed obvious: any ailments "cured" at these services were imaginary; any "healings" received, purely psychological. I granted that there was a strong possibility of psychotherapeutic benefit resulting from such "healing" services—that is, if people did not go overboard and refuse medical care—and I would concede that certain types of psychosomatic ailments might respond favorably to this type of psychosomatic treatment, but that any true organic or congenital disease could be healed through a church service was manifestly absurd.

Later I lunched with my doctor, a close personal friend. Towards the end of the meal, he made some reference to my new neighbors, who were also his patients. "Remarkable recovery that child made," he said. "We'd done all we could do for her medically. Scientifically speaking, she didn't have a chance—but now she's fully recovered. You could almost say it was a miracle."

I good-naturedly chided him, a medical man, for his choice of the word "miracle."

"That's about the only word you can use in a case like this," he commented dryly, "and this is not by any means the first I've seen."

I told him, then, of my involuntary attendance at the healing service. He nodded, then went on to relate several medically inexplicable healings that had occurred among his patients, including one apparently instantaneous healing of a carefully diagnosed, inoperable cancer.

"I saw a woman day before yesterday who was scheduled to go in for a goiter operation today. She went to a service last week, and claimed her goiter spontaneously disappeared. All I know is, there wasn't a sign of it when I examined her two days ago."

I looked up, startled. "Was she a small woman, dark eyes and hair? Did she wear a gray coat with a large fur collar?" The doctor nodded. "Yes. Mrs. J. She lives down the street from you. Do you know her?"

"I sat beside her when she was healed," I said.

The excitement I felt is hard to describe. I was still skeptical. The best doctors can be mistaken. However, if a medical man of good reputation dared acknowledge these healing phenomena, there could be something to it.

One thing was sure: It would make a whale of a story if there were any facts at all to back it up. I decided then and there to do some investigating.

The Reporter Investigates

My first step was to attend a number of healing services in various churches, in order to make sure that the apparent healings were occurring on a sufficiently wide scale to justify even a cursory investigation. At the end of two months, I was satisfied that alleged healings were occurring in many different churches, and I was anxious to explore what appeared to be an extensive phenomenon.

In contacting those local clergy who practiced the healing ministry, I freely acknowledged that I was not a believer. Without equivocation I stated my purpose: As a reporter I was out to prove or disprove the validity of some of the many healings being claimed. I found both clergy and laity undismayed by my skepticism and unafraid of my proposed investigation. Not only were they willing to cooperate, but most exerted considerable time and effort in helping me to procure the type of unimpeachable evidence I required.

That this evidence was going to be difficult to obtain was obvious from the start. Hospital medical records are not available to the patient or to anyone else without cooperation of both the hospital and the doctor in charge. This joint cooperation was always difficult and frequently impossible to procure. However, laboratory reports indicating the patient's former condition and attesting to subsequent improvement or cure following an alleged spiritual healing provided impressive substantiation of the claimed nonmedical cures.

When these medical reports were unavailable, the doctor in charge was asked to confirm the original diagnosis and any subsequent change in the patient's condition. A number of doctors complied with this request very cautiously. For example, one physician had examined a woman for whom an operation was scheduled. His written report stated that her bladder had dropped, causing it to protrude through her vagina. Eight days later, after her claimed healing, he reexamined her and reported in writing: "The patient was found to be much improved." In the interest of accuracy, it should be stated that the woman had been entirely healed, and the scheduled operation was canceled.

Many doctors refused to issue even so cautious a statement as the one just quoted. Some were willing to give me a written statement as to the present condition of the patient, but only a verbal acknowledgment of the original diagnosis.

A number of physicians preferred still another approach. They were willing to confirm their original diagnosis but refused to state that any type of healing had occurred. However, in those cases where the patient's cure was perceptible even to the most casual observer, I accepted as trustworthy evidence the original diagnosis and the patient's obvious lack of symptoms.

In cases involving surgery, the patient's story as to operative procedure and medical findings was verified wherever possible by the participating doctors. In some such cases the testimonies of clergy, friends, family, and outside agencies constituted an authoritative contribution to the healing picture.

Some doctors claimed a mistaken diagnosis, and at times this certainly seemed a plausible explanation. But in other instances, taking into account the number and variety of diagnostic tests, the sudden remission of all previous symptoms, the dramatic physical change from one desperately ill to one in glowing health, this explanation appeared to me suspiciously inadequate.

Now I have a profound admiration for the medical profession, but by the time I had examined some twenty similar cases, I began to grow irritated with the profession's monotonous refrain, "Wrong diagnosis." I finally pointed out to one of these doctors that he and his coworkers were indicting the medical profession for criminal incompetency. For within a few weeks, I had encountered nearly two dozen cases where the mistake in diagnosis could have permanently disabled the patient by drastic and unnecessary surgery or could have caused the patient's death.

Workmen's compensation reports and similar documents have provided reliable proof of the genuineness of a former ailment. Time after time I saw cases like that of the man who sustained an injury as the result of an accident at work, suffering the total loss of use of one of his limbs. After careful examination by six doctors who testified to his permanent disability, he was awarded full compensation, but was able to resume strenuous physical labor after his healing, with full use of the disabled limb restored. This constituted, in my eyes, incontrovertible evidence of his recovery.

As time went on, the variety of evidence attesting to former illness and medically unlikely cure left little doubt in my mind that some extraordinary healing force was in operation. Also, many cases of medically inexplicable recoveries were submitted to me by doctors.

Take, for example, the boy involved in an automobile accident. He was thrown out of the car, which landed on top of him. His back was crushed, and he was bleeding profusely and extensively. Taken to a nearby hospital, he lay unconscious for many weeks, paralyzed from the neck down. According to the doctors, his case was completely hopeless. The only person still hopeful was his minister, who went each day to the hospital to pray for him. At last the boy regained consciousness, and the clergyman confidently expressed his conviction that God would heal him. The doctors were extremely critical, objecting that it was barbaric cruelty to assure an obviously hopeless case of recovery.

One day, about two weeks after the patient had emerged from the coma, he received the laying-on of hands and felt a sensation like "liquid fire running through [his] body." Three weeks later he got out of bed and walked. He reentered college the next fall and graduated a year later with highest honors.

Scores of such verifiable healings, reported by reputable doctors, induced me to believe that these healings were not mere happenstance. At the end of a few months I noted that this strange healing force worked in curiously different ways. Some healings occurred through prayer for a patient miles away. Some were instant and complete; others were delayed and gradual. In most cases of spiritual healing, the defective organ supposed to cause the illness was restored to normal function, but in a few cases the individual attained complete health in spite of the fact that the condition of the organ remained ostensibly unchanged.

Several cases were brought to my attention of that amazing manifestation of the healing force that results in the physical evidence of surgery, though none has taken place. In one instance, for example, a woman was spiritually healed of a breast tumor. Immediately after her healing, a scar became visible.

In an effort to shed some light on the healing phenomenon, I searched continuously for some evidence of a general, underlying psychic factor—some common quality of personality, perhaps, that might make those healed peculiarly susceptible to the healing power—whatever it was and wherever it came from. I could find no such common denominator. Those healed came from every walk of life. They were of varying degrees of intelligence and different levels of education. They were of many diverse temperaments. Only after the healings was there a discernible common bond: a joyous faith in God, founded on the conviction shared by factory worker and professional alike, that God's mysteries cannot be intellectualized.

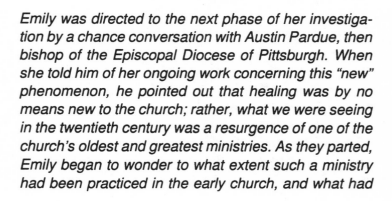

Emily was directed to the next phase of her investigation by a chance conversation with Austin Pardue, then bishop of the Episcopal Diocese of Pittsburgh. When she told him of her ongoing work concerning this "new" phenomenon, he pointed out that healing was by no means new to the church; rather, what we were seeing in the twentieth century was a resurgence of one of the church's oldest and greatest ministries. As they parted, Emily began to wonder to what extent such a ministry had been practiced in the early church, and what had

caused it to lie essentially dormant for many centuries. The following is her account of healing in the early church and reasons for the gradual corruption and decline of this essential Christian ministry.

The great healing ministry of the Christian church actually began in the New Testament with the Book of Acts, which records some thirteen clear-cut physical healings after Christ's ascension. However, we are not dependent on the word-of-mouth "fables," as some term them, of the New Testament. Through the prolific writings of the early Christians, we are able to follow closely, by means of eyewitness reports, the history of healing in the church through the first three centuries after Christ. During these three hundred years, the healing of the body was a vitally important function of the church.

The writings of the early church upon which the evidence is based are clearly not the emotional outpourings of religious fanatics. They are, rather, meticulous records, prepared by intelligent and highly educated theologians who were fully aware that their work would probably be exposed to merciless investigation by the Roman authorities. Irenaeus, Tertullian, Origen, Justin Martyr, and many others too numerous to mention have marshalled impressive evidence regarding spiritual healing in the early church.

Tertullian, a Christian convert, later to become one of the church's greatest theologians, cites numerous instances of physical healings in his writings. In his *On the Flesh of Christ*, written about A.D. 200, he tells specifically of healings of leprosy, blindness, and palsy, and makes frequent mention of the raising of the dead.

Origen, both teacher and writer and one of the greatest thinkers of the early Christian church, offers convincing evidence of the prevalence of physical healings in his work *Against Celsus,* written in the third century.

One of the greatest single sources of information concerning miraculous healings lies in a treatise called *Against Heresies,* written about A.D. 170 by Irenaeus, an eminent Greek churchman in Gaul. In this work, the author deals at length and in detail with the healings, which "occur daily," of blindness, leprosy, and deafness, as well as the raising of the dead: "The entire church entreating that boon with much fasting and prayer."

This is what others say: "And one is cured, receiving healing by faith; and the dead is raised up in consequence of the power of one believing that he would be raised," says Clement of Alexandria in the first century.

"In the Name of Jesus Christ, our Christian men have healed and do heal," exclaims Justin Martyr in the second century.

"The Name of Jesus repels demons and takes away disease," states Origen in the third century.

We are assured again and again that through prayer, implemented by the laying-on of hands, holy anointing, exorcism in the name of Jesus Christ, and the sign of the cross, these healings were being received by the faithful—healings so numerous and so miraculous that even the Roman authorities were obliged to confirm them.

Throughout all the writings of the early Christians runs the same recurrent theme: No disease can remain impervious to the power of the Holy Spirit; for all who believe, this power is abundantly available.

But can we really believe the writings of these early Christian teachers, philosophers, and theologians, or is the evidence they present the fabrication of over-stimulated imaginations, the product of overzealous hearts?

After a concentrated study of their reasoned and scholarly expositions, I can only reasonably conclude that such unanimity of experience as reported by so many honest and intelligent men, at different times and from different places, constitutes reliable historical evidence, fully as worthy of credence as the data compiled by any other historians, upon whose written word we have necessarily based our knowledge of history.

It is abundantly clear that the great healing ministry of Christ was, in the post-apostolic days, and according to his command, channeled and manifested through his Body, the church. The power of God was a living reality to thousands of the faithful. Eyewitness accounts, including those of Ignatius, martyred in A.D. 177, relate numerous instances of those martyrs who were thrown to wild beasts and emerged unscathed; of those persecuted who endured the most unspeakable torture, yet felt no pain, protected as they were by the invulnerable armor of their faith in the near presence of their Lord.

What happened, then, to this great healing and protective power? Why, at the beginning of the fourth century, did St. Augustine refer to miracles as being most unusual and apparently becoming increasingly rare?

Reflecting on the recorded events of that period, I believe that the decline is attributable to increasing controversy within the church and to the church's position of conflict with emerging medical science. The once-united church had become split by controversy and was no longer steadfast in the faith. Much as it is today, it was floundering in the morass of conflicting opinion, and inevitably there occurred a weakening of spiritual power and of the people's faith. It became a vicious cycle: as the church's faith weakened, so did the power of healing; and as healing declined, the faith that remained was further diminished.

Faith is always a tenuous, ephemeral thing, and it is never easy. Even for the disciples, with Jesus beside them, it was hard to retain. Small wonder, then, that gradually, almost imperceptibly, the glowing faith left by Christ and replenished by the Holy Spirit should have dwindled.

As she lost her power to heal, the church rationalized that God's will was for humanity to suffer. Thus began the heresy that God wills disease and sends it as a means of punishment for his recalcitrant children.

Simultaneously medical practice was moving out of the monasteries, where it was first largely developed, and moved progressively into the secular realm. The church, however, refused to accept the proven scientific truths pertaining to disease and its prevention. By obstructing medical science at every turn, the church unwittingly began the conflict that is only now beginning to be resolved.

Not realizing that God is responsible for all healing, no matter what the method, people began to transfer their allegiance from the church to medicine, from God to drugs. Incidentally, taking a pill was easier then, as it is now, than the faith and true repentance that are necessary for spiritual healing.

Thus the dark ages of the healing ministry began in

the fourth century, when the dynamic faith of the early Christians degenerated into prosaic lip service. Divided by schism and mistakenly resisting medical science, the church allowed her ministry of healing to fade into the background, where it was largely hidden, although never completely lost. Pondering these conclusions, I began to find it credible that the healings taking place today might mean the renascence of the ancient and powerful healing ministry.

Could it be, I dared to ask myself, that these miracles were not merely a scientific phenomenon, but instead a direct and purposeful manifestation of the power of God? I was awed at the thought and considerably embarrassed to be harboring it. I wasn't quite ready as yet to go all the way with the Holy Spirit theory. However, very cautiously, and strictly to myself, I had to admit the possibility that those who believe might have some logical basis for their faith.

Facing the Evidence

It is a strange human perversity that while we seek, often with near-desperation, demonstrable evidence that God exists, we do everything in our power to discredit that evidence when confronted by it. We are, generally speaking, willing to render unto Caesar what is Caesar's, but we will fight to the last ditch against rendering unto God what is God's. I was no exception. No agnostic ever tried more assiduously than I to disprove what seemed to me the fantastic notion that God miraculously healed the sick.

Because I believe that my own reactions to the question of spiritual healing were in many respects typical, I would like to detail here a few of the arguments I propounded in my effort to explain away the phenomenon.

I founded my case primarily on the premise that miracles are not admissible in the world of science. With no scientific basis for their existence, they therefore could not be. It was some time before I realized that many of us apply variable standards regarding scientific "proof." Take the case of a man dying of pneumonia. He is given a shot of penicillin, then recovers. His friends and relatives exclaim, "Thank heaven for penicillin! It saved his life!" They don't lie awake nights thinking up reasons why penicillin had nothing whatsoever to do with his recovery.

"Of course not," you retort, as did I. "The effectiveness of penicillin against pneumonia has been scientifically proven."

Exactly. But take, then, the case of a man dying of an inoperable cancer. His ailment has been diagnosed by modern scientific laboratory procedure—the accuracy of which has been as incontestably proved as the efficacy of penicillin against pneumonia. The cancer victim is spiritually healed and what happens? When confronted with the fact of his recovery, our faith in science inexplicably flies out the window. We are suddenly and unalterably convinced that X-rays lie, and microscopes deceive. "Wrong diagnosis!" we shout. And for a long time my voice led all the rest.

There is no doubt that a particular individual may have received a wrong diagnosis. There is always a human margin of error, no matter what the actual scientific method. X-rays can be misread and the microscopic analysis of tissue can be misinterpreted, but only in isolated instances—not time after time. As the evidence mounted, bearing witness to the fact that an extremely large number of scientifically diagnosed incurables were being healed, it eventually seemed to me that there was only one of two logical conclusions to be derived from the facts: either these so-called incurable cases were being healed by an outside force, or an appalling number of doctors are charlatans and modern diagnostic techniques are worthless.

I chose the former explanation as the more rational. I simply do not believe that doctors in general are criminally incompetent, nor are the procedures they use entirely untrustworthy. In recognition, then, of the illogical conclusions to which my logical reasoning had led me, I was forced, in honesty, to repudiate the "wrong diagnosis" theory.

As my investigations progressed, my carefully manufactured explanations, calculated to deny God's healing power, fell by the wayside. I had, of course, toyed briefly with the "imaginary" illness idea. Surely, I argued, the ailments for which cures had been claimed were purely imaginary. Investigation revealed, however, that although a few suffering from apparently nonexistent ailments had claimed "cures," these were distinctly in the minority. The vast majority, according to scientific evidence, have suffered disabilities that were indeed real.

A forty-year-old woman, whose doctor has testified she has no eardrums, suddenly hears for the first time in her life. Had she, with no eardrums, merely imagined that she could not hear before? A blind man suddenly regains his sight. It is a matter of public record that, twenty years before, his cornea had been destroyed by a splinter of molten steel. Had he merely imagined that he could not see before?

Scores of similar cases caused my theory of imaginary illness to topple.

Next I explored the "previous medical treatment" theory. I knew that most of the cases seeking spiritual healing had been medically treated for years, apparently without result. Could it be, I wondered, that those patients who thought themselves "spiritually" healed were in reality experiencing a delayed response to their earlier medical care? Within a month I was forced to discard this hypothesis as invalid. There is no doubt that such a thing might happen occasionally, but it just didn't make sense that time after time the response, delayed for years, should suddenly occur in the middle of a healing service.

By this time, it seemed impossible to explain away the healings I was witnessing. Nonetheless, I was a long way from accepting the Holy Spirit explanation so glibly offered by those healed. The answer, I told myself, must lie in science—and here I was right back where I had started months before. By this time I was convinced that a higher scientific law, of which we were ignorant, was in operation. What was happening must be some sort of scientific phenomenon.

With this explanation I was more or less content—until I began to take note of what was happening to the lives of those who had been healed. A man, who as the result of a hopeless spinal injury was doomed to a life of complete invalidism and intolerable pain, was healed instantly. Resuming his former job at a mill, he promptly started weekly prayer meetings with his working companions.

A man, who for years had gambled away his earnings and abused his family, felt the Lord's healing touch. He turned to God, gave up gambling, and is now a model husband and father.

A wealthy, spoiled woman, having felt the healing power, now gives unstintingly of her wealth and time and energy to assist in setting up healing missions all over the country.

And there are scores of run-of-the-mill people, like you and me, neither particularly good nor particularly bad, who, having been healed, work unceasingly with grateful hearts and eager hands so that others, too, may know what they have discovered.

Was all of this coincidence? No, for I found that the inspiring stories of changed lives were as numerous as those healed.

After talking to over a hundred of these people, I began, at last, to comprehend the true significance of their healings. It gradually became clear to me that spiritual healing, achieved through faith in God and in the promises of his Son, Jesus Christ, has one purpose only—the soul's salvation. The physical healing was incidental—only a small part of the healing of the whole person. Wonderful and dramatic as it is that the blind see, and the deaf hear, and the crippled take up their beds and walk, it is far more wonderful, and infinitely more exciting, to witness the spiritual regeneration that seemed inevitably to follow the healing of the body.

The changed lives and glowing faces of those I have seen healed are surely the outward and visible signs of an inward and spiritual grace. Their healthy bodies and renewed lives, dedicated to the glory of God, would seem to bear indisputable witness to the fact that God lives. An inner radiance seems to flood their faces, often lending to their features an almost luminous appearance. It was my noting of this phenomenon, again and again, which was to lead me to believe.

Not long ago I had dinner with an executive of a large corporation whom I knew to be a freethinker. During the course of the meal, a man healed of lung cancer, whom I had interviewed some months before, stopped at our table. I introduced him to my friend, we spoke briefly, and the man went on his way.

I turned back to my dinner companion to resume our interrupted conversation, and I saw his glance follow the man to the door. He turned to me with a look of bewilderment on his face. "Who was that man?" he asked. "Did you notice that strange glow he had, or am I crazy?"

I explained briefly—and for over an hour he bombarded me with eager questions. As we paid our bill, he remarked: "You know, I've always believed you were an honest reporter, but frankly, if I hadn't just seen that man, I'd be certain you had a screw loose. Having seen him, I'm not surprised at anything you've told me. Now don't get me wrong. I don't believe in this sort of thing, but that man has experienced something I don't know anything about. I'm just curious enough to want to learn more. How about dinner next week?"

As I look back now, I see that the first real assault on my own unbelief began on the day I was forced to concede that a great outside healing power was at work. Conferences with doctors, innumerable interviews, and a long and arduous study of the medical histories of hopelessly broken bodies now fully restored had left me no alternative explanation.

I was not able to define that power until I realized the healings extended far beyond the realm of the purely physical. The death knell of my skepticism was to sound when I grasped their true significance. It was then that I became convinced that the phenomenon was of God.

Of course, I do not know—perhaps no one who is only an observer can know—whether these miraculous healings are actually a direct and personal manifestation of the Holy Spirit. I can only state that in the opinion of an unbiased reporter honestly seeking the truth, the cumulative evidence indicates that this healing power is not an unknown scientific law called, for some mysterious reason, into startling operation, but that it is the direct intervention of the Holy Spirit in our lives—the evidence we have long sought of a living God.

Emily's Credo

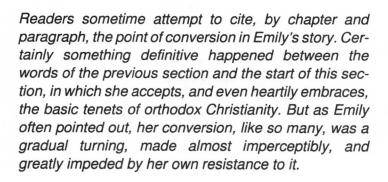

Readers sometime attempt to cite, by chapter and paragraph, the point of conversion in Emily's story. Certainly something definitive happened between the words of the previous section and the start of this section, in which she accepts, and even heartily embraces, the basic tenets of orthodox Christianity. But as Emily often pointed out, her conversion, like so many, was a gradual turning, made almost imperceptibly, and greatly impeded by her own resistance to it.

By this time, I was committed to far more than a belief in spiritual healing. I was irrevocably committed to the doctrine of Jesus Christ as proclaimed by the church.

Had I been an agnostic before? I certainly had not considered myself such. If anyone had asked me whether I believed in God, I would have replied, Yes. If anyone had asked whether I were a Christian, my answer would likewise have been in the affirmative. I see now that I would unwittingly have been committing perjury, for the truth of the matter was that, to me, God was merely a convenient abstraction, while Christianity consisted of abiding, in so far as was practicable, by the golden rule. Oh, I had searched once, years ago, for a more satisfactory, a more personal concept, but I had not found it. I had long since grown weary of the search. "Seek and ye shall find" had lost any personal significance. It was a well-phrased slogan, applicable to everything except religion.

For some, faith comes easily. In my ignorance, I had thought that those who could obey the command "Follow thou me" without question were unthinking, rather stupid people. I know now that they are the inestimably blessed. For others, like myself, the acquisition of real faith is a difficult and often acutely painful process: a war between mind and heart. But if years ago I had managed to rationalize myself out of belief, I was now, through my interest in spiritual healing, to reason myself into faith.

I was neither healed of any physical disability nor was I, in the usual sense, converted. But in seeking an explanation for the phenomenon of nonmedical healings, I was forced into an analysis of Christianity.

I had long considered the basic, church-held concept of Jesus Christ impossible to believe, and then I stumbled, as I think now, with purpose, onto the phenomenon of spiritual healing.

The whole thing fell into place like the pieces of a jigsaw puzzle when I finally selected what seemed to me the more logical of two basic premises: Either Christianity is the greatest hoax ever perpetrated, or the great tenets of the Christian faith are eternal and unchangeable truth. I could find no evidence to substantiate the first contention, but I believe there is demonstrable proof of the validity of the latter. On this I base my own personal case for Christianity.

I had called myself a Christian, but I had never taken the time or trouble to decipher either the meaning or the implication of Christianity. Perhaps this was because I was guilty of the cowardice I think the modern church has fostered—the fear of believing too much, which results so often in believing nothing at all. Perhaps it was because at that time I could not or would not hurdle the stumbling blocks inherent in the gospels—stumbling blocks caused not by the things I didn't understand in the New Testament, but by the things I did understand but didn't want to believe.

I laughed off, for instance, the doctrine of original sin. "He is the propitiation for our sins." What sins? I hadn't done anything to be ashamed of!

I denied Jesus' divinity. After all, this is an enlightened age. The supernatural is intellectually unacceptable. Then I realized that either he was the Son of God as he claimed, or a prodigious liar and dangerous psychopath whose teachings should be relegated to obscurity as the ravings of a madman.

I repudiated the miracles, obviously mere fantasy: myths perpetrated by overenthusiastic gospel writers. I gradually awoke to the fact that if I denied those miracles, I must, in consistency, deny the Resurrection. And just where does that leave Christianity?

To take literally the origin and destiny of Jesus and even most of his teaching was stretching credulity too far. I would not go beyond my admission that he was a good man and a great teacher. But one must differentiate between what was practical and what was hopeless idealism, obviously not intended for present-day living. Turn the other cheek? Give him who had stolen my coat, my cloak also? Surely no one could take this sort of teaching seriously!

Oh, I believed parts of the New Testament. I was heartily in favor of spreading Christianity. It was a fine ethical and moral code. I was ready to go along with Jesus' command to preach the Kingdom of God, but I took it upon myself (supported by most of the churches) to peremptorily dismiss the second portion of the command, to "heal the sick" (Luke 9:2).

"Go ye into all the world and preach the gospel to every living creature" seemed a pretty good idea, but just let's forget the rest of it, when he said, in no uncertain terms: "And these signs shall follow them that believe . . . they shall lay hands on the sick, and they shall recover" (Mark 16:17-18).

It took a long time, but eventually I became convinced of the fallacy of this sort of unauthoritative selective belief. It seemed to me that wherever it was indulged in, spiritual strength was dissipated and the cause of Christianity weakened.

They say that faith is more a matter of the heart than

of the mind, and this is essentially true. But there is a vast difference between *belief* and *faith*, even though the one almost invariably follows the other. *Belief* is the mind's acceptance, and *faith* is the heart's receiving. My heart was to remain locked until my mind could accept Christ.

My faith came not as a sudden and dramatic conversion, but by means of a rather torturously-arrived-at intellectual conviction. To me, Christianity made good sense, but to derive the sense from it, I must believe all that Christ taught or I must believe none of it. Christianity is not a myth. It is an historical and clearly definitive religion; there are no halfway measures. I feel that neither I, a lay woman, nor any theologian, however learned, can choose at random and select without authority what is convenient for the one to believe and interesting for the other to teach. If we take it upon ourselves to do so, we are degrading Christianity into a fabricated code of half-truths, and the step from a half-truth to a lie is notoriously short.

It is my opinion that if we casually overlook, interpret away, or attempt to make more palatable the difficult teachings of our Lord, we are degrading Christianity into a chaotic and untrustworthy cult. To me, either the whole thing is true, or the whole thing is false. You make your choice. I made mine on the basis of the results of true Christian faith as I saw them first, in spiritual healing of the body, and as I have recognized them since, in spiritual healing of the soul. My mind's acceptance proved the key that was to open my heart to full faith.

I repudiated my background, which for so long had conditioned me against literal Christianity. I reversed my former beliefs and corrected my former misapprehensions, such as my belief that religion was for the weak. I knew now that our strength can be computed by the degree to which we depend on God, while our courage can be determined by the extent to which we dare to claim Christ's promises.

I was ready at last to confess a living God and his only begotten Son, Jesus Christ, who was sent to redeem the world.

The Will of God

———◆———

When Emily accepted with both mind and heart the basic orthodox beliefs of the Christian faith, her works took a new direction. She began to function not only as a reporter, giving accounts of the healings she was witnessing, but as a teacher, addressing some of the major theological issues involved in the church's healing ministry. One principal issue she dealt with was the will of God for humankind, and the problem posed by sickness, pain, and evil in the world.

———◆———

The problem of pain in relation to a compassionate and almighty God is a difficult one. Throughout the ages it has puzzled far abler minds than mine. Small wonder then that it proved for me, as it has for so many, one of Christianity's greatest hurdles.

For a while I was ready to give up on it and take the easy way out: Assume that God did send disease and suffering, and accept as fact that writhing bodies were God-sent crucibles to ensure spiritual purification. And then I saw a good, courageous man in the prime of life, dying by inches, in agony; an agony that seemed to supersede mind or spirit, an agony that reduced him to the level of a wounded jungle animal for whom pain was the only reality. His eyes glazed with the now-ineffective morphine, he gasped a week before he died, "It's lucky I did my praying before. I can't concentrate now on anything except the pain."

Once again my old rebellion flared. Love a God whose love for his children included inflicting upon them the tortures of the damned? I knew that many Christians professed love for such a God. Then they were made of sterner stuff than I.

What, then, was the answer? I turned again to Scripture. As I reread the gospels, I wondered briefly if I were completely on the wrong track. Could it be that our ideas of "love" and "good" were wholly different from God's? And then I came to our Lord's own words: "If ye then, being evil, know how to give good gifts unto your children, how much more shall your Father which is in heaven give good things to them that ask him?" (Matt. 7:11). I had my answer.

I thought again of the healings. It simply didn't make sense that God would go against his own will by curing the sick. I saw in Jesus' life a saga of his unremitting labor to assuage and eradicate human pain. Would he, who so often proclaimed, "I and my Father are one," work ceaselessly against his Father's will?

Although we may never know the full answer to the why of pain, we hold in our knowledge, however incomplete, the most vital essence of a great Christian truth: God does not will or send the diseases crippling so many here on earth.

Now comes the inevitable question. If God does not will suffering, and yet permits it, how can God be omnipotent? The answer to this is not simple, any more than Christianity itself is simple. But although "we must trust in the Lord with all our hearts, and lean not unto our own understanding," I believe that the question need not be intellectually circumvented. It can, in my opinion, be met head-on, and at least a partial explanation found.

Christianity acknowledges a state of war between good and evil—a battle between two forces, the one led by God and the other by Satan. Satan can never triumph over God, for to the Creator must go the ultimate victory, but he can hinder and temporarily delay the perfect execution of God's will for us.

In shedding fundamentalism, some have shrugged off the concept of the devil, but an increasing number of advanced thinkers are returning to it as the most logical explanation of suffering and evil in a world created good. We have smiled at the biblical idea of the devil, discarding it as childish fantasy as we have discarded so many other Christian tenets. Yet the concept of Satan can help as we try to deal with the fact of evil in this world.

Throughout the New Testament, we read of a dark power, an evil spirit, who was held to be the power behind sin and its concomitants, disease and death. Thus the Epistle to the Ephesians reads, "Put on the whole armor of God, that ye may be able to stand against the wiles of the devil. For we wrestle not against flesh and blood, but against principalities, against powers, against the rulers of the darkness of this world" (Eph. 6:11-12). To Jesus, Satan was a very real and formidable adversary during his temptation in the wilderness. The devil "departed from him for a season," but he was to return and plague Christ's disciples as he does us. "Simon, Simon, behold, Satan hath desired to have you . . . but I have prayed for thee, that thy faith fail not" (Luke 22:31-32).

It is interesting to note that those who have been closest to Christ, from his disciples to the modern saints, have been the most convinced of the reality of Satan. The stories of their lives reveal their unremitting battle against the evil spirits.

Now, you may not believe in an actual devil, but I think most will agree that there seem to be powers of evil opposing God's perfect will for the world, deflecting it from its intention. This does not mean that God is not almighty. God chose to create us with free will (which we often misuse) rather than as automatons, guaranteed to carry out his plan for us. It seems to me that much of our confusion regarding God's omnipotence is due to our human, and therefore finite, interpretation of the word *almighty*. God is almighty in love and power. Slowly but surely, he conquers the evil force. God's triumph will ultimately be complete.

Although the kingdom of God is not entirely beyond this world, neither is it wholly realizable here on earth. Christianity assures us that God will conquer sin and evil, but in God's own way and time. This way may be, for us humans, incomprehensible, but this does not mean that God is withholding from those of us now on earth all knowledge of the Kingdom. In many ways, perhaps most dramatically through physical healings and spiritual regeneration, he is giving us a foretaste of the kingdom, here and now.

If God's will for us is perfect and abundant health, what about death? Isn't the deterioration of bodily tissues inevitable as part of creation?

There is sharp division of opinion on this matter. Some theologians theorize that deterioration of tissue is not part of God's creation, but came about as a result of the Fall. They claim that physical death is not a "natural" process, but a punishment for sin. "Death ceases in the world when the sin of the world dies."

It is possible that God's original plan for the world, had it been unhampered by sin, might have excluded death of the body. But here we are clearly in the realm of pure conjecture. We simply do not know. What we do know, however, is that God does not will humanity to suffer.

In this discussion of God's will, I have not overlooked the fact that many of the saints accepted the theory that God sends suffering as a means of spiritual growth. They saw in their own afflictions a means of increasing their spiritual stature, and they used it to the fullest extent. And in many cases, this is true today. Although pain is often apt to be a demoralizing, sterile thing, forcing concentration on the body to the exclusion of the soul, it is not always wasted. There are many Christians who heroically endure pain with incredible courage, using it to strengthen them spiritually and bring them closer to God. They are magnificently proving the truth of Christ's saying that in our endurance, we win possession of our souls.

Nevertheless, however able we may be to convert the evil of suffering to a holy purpose, the pain itself did not emanate from God. If we can use it to his glory, we indeed know triumph over the evil spirits. But this does not alter the fact that God did not create the evil of suffering. He has simply overcome it.

Emily addresses the question of the will of God in each of her books on healing, stating that "the basic premise on which the healing ministry rests is that sickness is not the will of God." In The Lord Is Our Healer *she notes the inconsistency of the position we so often take concerning the medical treatment of illness.*

If you sincerely feel that God wills your sickness, then, if you are a Christian striving to do his will, you must, to be consistent, reject all medical treatment. Your purpose in receiving it is obviously to be healed, and thus you are deliberately working against God's will as you conceive it to be.

It is a sort of Christian schizophrenia when we profess to believe that sickness is the will of God, and then when sickness strikes, rush to call the best doctor available. It is, in effect, splitting our personalities down the middle, with one belief for religious use, and an antithetical one for our secular lives.

This schizophrenic situation is sharply emphasized by our ostensible worship of a "good" God: the "Father of all mercies, and the God of all comfort" (2 Cor. 1:3); a Father whose "good pleasure it is to give you the kingdom" (Luke 12:32); a Father who "knoweth what

43

things ye have need of, before ye ask him" (Matt. 6:8). And yet any catastrophe that befalls us we glibly declare to be the "will of God." (H24)

Emily repeatedly urges us to see that because illness is not God's will, it is something to be fought in the same way that we fight the temptation to sin. Here are two of her typical calls to battle.

Most of us are probably all too familiar with the necessity of resisting temptation (as well as the results if we do not), but the idea of resisting disease as also evil comes as a new idea to many of us. The battle is not always easy, in either case, and it requires considerably more faith and effort than sitting passively by and saying, "Thy will be done." But if you believe that disease, like sin, is evil, you will find yourself compelled to combat the one as fiercely as the other so that God's will may indeed be done. The result is often a miracle of healing. (NI53)

Christianity is not an easy faith, and our Lord never said it was—and it is no easier in the area of disease than in the realm of sin. It demands that we do not resign ourselves to either, but fight the one as vigorously as the other, convinced that neither is the will of God—and equally convinced that if we fight the good fight, our battle spoils will include healing as well as forgiveness. (H26)

CHAPTER TWO

Discovering the Healing Power

———◆———

In her journalism Emily had experienced the freedom of reporters and freelance writers, who can turn their backs on each assignment when the story reaches print. The desk was clear, and a new topic beckoned. This time, though, Emily found that she could not abandon the subject of spiritual healing. "One does not walk away," she said, "from tangible evidence of the power of God."

So she continued to investigate and record the many cases of spiritual healing she encountered. She now documented case histories, not to disprove a premise but to prove one. Believing that much harm is done to the healing ministry by false or careless claims, Emily continued making every effort to confirm medically as many healings as possible. This investigative work, coupled with ever-deepening study of Scripture and theology, led to her second book, God Can Heal You Now *(1958). In this, as in all her books, what Emily had seen was passed on to her readers in the form of case histories to illustrate what she had learned. Her work as a reporter had trained her to notice and incorporate the human details that give life to a story. Because these accounts were so often deeply personal, Emily always respected the privacy of persons involved. So as to avoid any undesirable identification, she intentionally "scrambled" the healings and other incidents with respect to time and location. "The important thing," she said, "is that everything reported happened under the exact circumstance described."*

With the growing popularity of A Reporter Finds God, *Emily was invited often to speak at meetings and conferences. She led her first healing mission in 1957 in Wisconsin; there, unexpectedly, she was asked to minister with clergy behind the altar rail. Uncertain about the limits of her participation as a lay person, and, as always, respecting the authority of the church, she telephoned her bishop to ask what to do. He responded, "Do what you are told." Thus she found herself functioning for the first time not as an observer, reporter, author, lecturer, or teacher, but as a minister of God's healing grace through the laying-on of hands.*

Emily's new ministry was effective, and the results were apparent. She soon became known as a "healer" and sometimes, to her dismay, as a "faith healer." Certain connotations of that term, she felt, were inimical to both the theology and tradition of the church's ministry of healing. Her books began to reflect the experiences arising from her new role: healing missioner, leader of healing services and—to the extent possible—minister to the many individuals who sought her personal help.

The selections given here from Emily's second book deal in depth with three basic aspects of the healing ministry—faith, repentance, and love—and also with the sacramental healing rites of the church. Accompanying them are pertinent writings on these topics from Emily's other books.

Faith

Wherever you are, whoever you may be, the healing power of God is available to you today just as it was two thousand years ago. On the basis of what I have seen, I am wholly convinced that there is no disease so hopeless that it will not respond to God's almighty power, and no ailment so slight that it is unworthy of his healing love.

Once convinced that it is God's will that we should be well, our next step is to release his healing power so that it may flow through us unimpeded. Successful spiritual healing depends primarily on love, faith, and repentance. These three factors are interdependent, but faith might be called the core of spiritual healing, as it is of all Christianity. It is only when we believe Jesus Christ was the Son of God that we can accept the reality of his resurrective power in our lives today. It is only when we believe what Jesus told us of God that we can truly love our Creator. It is only when we believe what he told us of sin and its consequences that we can understand the necessity for repentance.

But no one knows better than I that this is easier said than done. The simple, childlike faith Christ demanded of his followers, and upon which he tells us depends our entry into the kingdom of heaven, is incredibly difficult for many of us to acquire in this day and age. I know it was for me; but I think now that had I known in the beginning what I have since learned, the road might have been less rough.

Not long ago someone said to me: "I only wish I had

your blind faith. But I'll never have that complete faith necessary for healing." This woman couched her comment diplomatically, but I knew exactly what she meant. I remember when I, too, used to envy people their "blind" faith. Yet at the same time, I felt distinctly superior that my intellect prevented my being so gullible as they. I have learned since that faith need not and should not be "blind."

While it is true that faith is trusting in some things that cannot be proved by scientific formula, it also calls for loyalty to all available evidence. My faith, then, is an acceptance of the evidence that God lives. This abundantly available evidence is to be found in the restored bodies and recreated spirits of those God has touched.

Complete faith unnecessary for healing

My friend was also mistaken in her assumption that complete faith is necessary for healing. I think that there is actually no such thing as complete faith. Fortunately for most of us, our healing does not depend on the amount of faith we have. Our Lord assures us that faith as small as a mustard seed can move mountains. It can also create healing miracles.

A young married woman was scheduled for radical surgery on a Tuesday morning. A biopsy had revealed a malignant tumor in her left breast. On the Friday preceding her operation, she attended a healing service at her church. "You could have fit my faith on a pinhead!" was the way she expressed it. "I really went only at the insistence of a friend."

During the service she felt a sensation "like electricity" streak across her chest, then center for an instant in her left breast. When she arose from the altar rail, she reports: "Never in my life have I had such a feeling of indescribable well-being and joy. I knew that something wonderful had happened to me inside. My friend said I had been healed, but just then it didn't seem to matter whether I had been physically cured or not."

That evening the young wife told her husband what had happened. "He just laughed," she said, "until he looked for the lump and found it gone." The next morning the couple went together to the doctor, who, after careful examination, declared that the growth seemed to have "mysteriously diminished in size." At his suggestion, however, she entered the hospital on schedule for another biopsy. The report came back negative. This woman's faith and that of countless others like her may have seemed less than a mustard seed, but it was enough for God to work through.

"Thy faith hath made thee whole" was the keynote of our Lord's earthly healing ministry. From what I have seen I believe that faith in some form is always necessary for healing today, although I am well aware that occasionally some are healed who appear to have no faith whatsoever.

Take the case of a man scheduled for surgery for a severe stomach ulcer, who frankly admits that he attended a healing service merely to please his wife. "Oh, I believed in God as an idea—an abstraction," he says, "but I had absolutely no faith in a personal God. Furthermore, I thought all this talk of miraculous healing was absolute bunk." Nevertheless, to his own stupefaction, the intense pain of his ulcer subsided as he knelt at the altar rail. A subsequent X-ray revealed that he was healed. No surgery was required.

Now this man himself may have lacked faith, but his

unbelief was routed by the massed faith of the believing worshipers who knelt beside him in the church. Here, of course, is the tremendous value of the church service. There is inestimable power in corporate faith. The almost palpable aura of expectant trust that characterizes a healing service not only increases the faith of the believers, but also seems to "rub off" on the unbelievers. If miracles are created through faith, faith, likewise, is created by miracles. Those healed do not remain unbelievers. They go on their way, like the once-blind beggar, "glorifying God."

Demanding personal faith

I think often of a religious conference I happened to attend. At the conference was a little woman, crippled from birth, who had long ago committed her life to Christ. She attended healing services regularly, praying always for others and that God would use her life for his glory.

I was greatly disturbed when at the conference I happened to overhear someone say to her, in a tone both condescending and arrogant, "If you really believed in God, you'd be healed. Look at me. I was healed because I had faith." Later that night, the devout and holy little woman came to me in tears. "But I do believe in God," she said, "and I know he can heal. Does the fact that I limp mean there's something wrong with my faith?"

After we talked for a while, we prayed together, and she left reassured. And that night I prayed fervently for the person who had made that remark. So much harm, so much unnecessary suffering, is caused by the ignorance and insensitivity of those who profess to be working in the name of Christ and witnessing for his sake.

Everyone who believes in the Lord Jesus is saved, but not all are physically healed. We do not know why, but we are sure that the failure is not necessarily due to a personal lack of deep faith. We base our certainty not only on teachings of the ancient church—which placed the responsibility for failure to heal on herself as the Body—but also on the Scripture from which this teaching was derived. For although our Lord frequently said to the one healed, "Thy faith hath made thee whole," he also healed the multitudes, many of whom, it is safe to assume, did not hold an intense personal faith. To be sure, he made clear that faith somewhere is necessary, whether it be the faith of friends, of the group as a whole, or of the one who ministers.

While we cannot ever underestimate the value of the faith of one who seeks healing, we must also note that Jesus did not always demand personal faith. He did not, for example, demand faith of Malchus when he healed the ear of the servant of the high priest (Luke 22:50-51), and it is highly unlikely that this man believed he would be healed. Nor did Jesus mention the faith of the man with palsy, brought by his friends (Mark 2:3-5). So crowded was the house where Jesus was that the sick man's friends could not get him near our Lord, so they let down the bed of the invalid through the roof. We are told that Jesus perceived the faith of these friends. And in healing the man with palsy, Jesus did not mention the man's faith (or lack of it), only the faith of his friends. (P91)

Exercising our faith

It is a fundamental psychological maxim that if people go through the proper motions, they soon begin to feel the corresponding emotions. So it is with faith. Go through the motions, exercise the faith you have, and your heart will react to receive God.

Attend healing services regularly. The church has become once more a vast reservoir of pentecostal power. Draw on this power. Let the healing church guide you, and the strength of corporate faith sustain and multiply your own. Seek out those who have felt God's touch, for the lamp of faith is lit, taper by taper, one from the other. Let them inspire and teach you. They have traveled the path before you and won their fight for faith.

Christ is with us at all times, but at the altar you will feel Christ's presence intensified. Hold up your cup of faith and he will fill it according to your ability to receive. (R117)

Persevering in faith

"Isn't it a lack of faith to continue to pray for healing after praying once and then committing oneself to God?"

The answer to this question is an emphatic no. Our Lord's admonition is to pray persistently—and to faint not. Again and again Jesus gives us parables to illustrate how God honors persevering prayer, such as the stories of the friend at midnight (Luke 11:5-8) and the importunate widow (Luke 18:1-8). Persevering prayer, far from denoting lack of faith, is an act of obedience to our Lord. Praying again and again in expectancy demonstrates not faltering, but rather an unshakable and unswerving faith in the goodness and mercy of God, who has assured us that whoever "cometh to me I will in no wise cast out" (John 6:37).

This coming to God is repeatedly emphasized

throughout the New Testament, and especially in the Lord's Prayer. Here we ask, "Give us this day our daily bread"; we don't pray once a year for a twelve months' supply. We cannot store up God's grace. We don't, for example, receive Holy Communion once in a lifetime, for we cannot bank the grace received. We partake of Christ's body and blood again and again.

In the healing ministry we respond to Christ's call, "Come unto me," on a continuous and continuing basis. (P89)

Faith in trying times

Our faith will not prevent all disaster, but it will defend us against disastrous consequences. It will not save us from all anguish, but it will give us dominion over pain. It will not spare us all grief, but it will enable us to triumph above it.

As committed Christians we may not know why tragedy has struck. It is enough that through it all we never lose our consciousness of the love and glory of God. We may not understand why the Crucifixion must invariably precede the Resurrection, but our fortitude lies in the knowledge that the sequence is inevitable—and our courage resides in the assurance that the one follows the other as surely as the night the day. (M53)

Repentance

Faith unlocks the door to God's power, but it is repentance that opens it.

"Thy sins are forgiven thee," Jesus said to the palsied man. "Arise, and take up thy couch" (Luke 5:20, 24).

"Confess your faults one to another . . . that ye may be healed," said James (James 5:16). Throughout the history of the church, healing and repentance have gone hand in hand.

"But surely you don't believe all that ridiculous stuff," said an old friend whom I hadn't seen for years. "What on earth has happened to your reason?"

"Yes, I do believe it now, and *because* of my reason. No one understands better than I, who was myself a skeptic so short a while ago, the difficulty of believing what Christ said, simply because he said it. But the healing ministry is based on this premise. Because I, with my own eyes, have seen the incredible power in Christ's words believed, the astounding results of his promises claimed, it seems to me now a clear-cut case of cause and effect: 'By their fruits shall ye know them'" (Matt. 7:16).

If we accept the validity of our Lord's mission, and practice what he tells us insofar as we can, we find the fruits of the faith. If we emasculate his teaching, selecting what we want to believe and rejecting what we would prefer to discard, we find ourselves left with a powerless ideology instead of a dynamic religion.

The subject of our own sin is one of those aspects of Christianity that most of us would probably like to forget, if not actively reject. But Christ teaches both the destructiveness of sin and the salvation of forgiveness. Repentance for our sins is an inextricable part of the healing ministry.

It is through repentance that we draw close to God. It is through God's absolving power that our souls are healed. During his earthly ministry, Jesus never refused his healing grace to a sinner, nor does he now. It is never the sin, only our lack of penitence, that blocks us from God.

What is sin?

"But what is sin?" a friend said to me in genuine bewilderment. "I haven't done anything wrong."

In his mind my friend, like a great many of us, associated sin with a concrete, nefarious act, like robbing a bank or committing a murder. In the sense of committing a criminal offense, he certainly hadn't "done" anything, but he had broken God's law. Just how he had done so was divulged during the course of our conversation.

Sin is disobedience to God, of which, in one way or another, we are all guilty. It is impossible to live a sinless life. Even in seemingly inconsequential things, such as eating too much or drinking too much, or smoking too much, which might appear to concern only ourselves, we are breaking the commandment "Love thy neighbor as thyself." We are harming our bodies—desecrating, if you will, the temple of the Holy Spirit.

The sins most frequently overlooked, however, are the sins of the spirit. Hostility, resentment, anger, fear, jealousy—these are the things that most flagrantly violate the law of love. To break this law is to commit an offense against God, and to suffer the consequences of physical disease as well as spiritual sickness.

Pride

The saints all put their finger on pride as the great spiritual culprit. As the most common of the sins, and the most dangerous because so insidious and far-reaching in its effects, it might not be too inaccurate to say that pride is actually behind, and responsible for, all sin. It leads to the exaltation of our own egos to the point where we worship ourselves and our achievements instead of the Creator of both. This tendency leads us into the greatest sin of all, a willful separation from God.

Pride has nothing to do with self-respect, which our Lord surely meant us to have and to maintain, or God would never have issued the second commandment. Pride means the sort of self-aggrandizement that precludes humility. Humility is the very basis of our relationship with God.

Without humility we cannot have true faith, for faith presupposes complete confidence in someone other than ourselves. Without humility we cannot love God, for love is a humble desire to please the loved one. It is lack of humility that makes us deny our need of penance. It is lack of humility that makes it so difficult not only to seek out our faults, but, having discovered them, to confess them. Whatever other virtues we may possess, if we do not have humility, we are lost; however grave our faults, if we are humble enough to confess them, we can be saved.

A woman who considered herself a pillar of the church suffered from seriously impaired vision from hardening of the arteries in the eyes. Her ophthalmologist declared that the damage done was irreversible, and his prognosis was eventual blindness. The patient, however, refused to accept this verdict as final. She knew too well the marvelous power of God to heal.

For some six months she sought spiritual healing through prayer and the sacramental healing rites of the church, with no result, physical or spiritual. "I couldn't understand it," she said. "I felt that there was a definite block in me hindering God's power, yet I couldn't put my finger on it. One day I sat down and really tried to think it through. I didn't smoke or drink like Mrs. S., who did both. I never missed a Sunday in church, and Mrs. X missed at least once a month. I gave twice as much to the church in time and money as did Mrs. T.

"Suddenly, as I went on in this vein to myself, I had the answer. It was my smugness—my self-righteousness —my intolerance—my pride that were to blame.

"Next day I went to the healing service, and for the first time in many years of churchgoing, I had a real sense of the sin I was asking to have forgiven. I received the laying-on of hands with the first honest humility I think I had ever felt. Kneeling there at the altar rail, I felt God's presence as I never had before."

Slowly but surely, this woman's vision improved. Today it is normal.

In the following excerpts Emily considers some of the difficulties in repentance and the question of guilt, showing once again the great harm that can be done by persons who minister insensitively. She discusses self-examination, modes of confession, and the paramount importance of accepting forgiveness.

Self-Examination

At first glance repentance would seem the easiest of the requisites of the faith to fulfill, but for me it has not proved so. It has often seemed incredibly difficult to make a wholly honest act of contrition. The problem of distinguishing between real penitence and a desire to realize God's benefits has been a very real one for me and, I have good reason to suspect, for many.

Two questions continually assailed me: Was I sorry merely because my sins were blocking me from God's power, or was I sorry because they had hurt Christ? Was I recognizing with my intellect alone, an error of omission or word or thought or deed, for which I knew I should be sorry, or was I truly seeking forgiveness of sin that I acknowledged with my heart as well as with my mind? It was when I fully realized everything depended on the answers to these questions that I adopted the practice of invariably preceding my prayer for forgiveness by a heartfelt prayer that I might honestly repent.

This was when I learned to pray, first with my lips, and finally with my heart: "Against thee, thee only have I sinned" (Ps. 51:4). This was when I learned that in response, a merciful God reaches down into the little hells we create for ourselves and makes "clean our hearts within us." This was when I learned that penitence is the result of God's grace and not our effort. I have been the grateful recipient of this grace times without number, and I have seen it frequently bestowed on the uncertain and confused.

Take, for example, the case of a woman who came to me a few months ago, wondering why she had not received healing. "I believe thoroughly that Christ heals," she said, "and I've been attending healing services for a year, but with no apparent benefit." She went on to explain that for several years before she had been engaged in an extramarital affair. "But that was all over a year ago," she said, "and I have asked God's forgiveness." Then anxiously she added: "You do think God has forgiven me, don't you?"

Before I had time to reply, she inadvertently supplied a clue to the problem. "Of course no one was hurt," she commented thoughtfully. "The affair just burned itself out, and my husband was never the wiser." The question then was not the forgiveness of God, which is never in doubt, but the sincerity of her contrition.

I sensed in her situation a dilemma that confronts many of us from time to time, whether our sin happens to be adultery or an explosive temper, selfishness or gossip, irritability or resentment. Had she confessed because she was genuinely sorry and longed to reestablish her relationship with God, or had she made an unintentionally empty gesture, because she now needed God's healing power? Had this woman subconsciously harbored the thought that once having achieved her desire—once having accomplished what she wanted to do—she would then, and only then, seek forgiveness? Given the same opportunity, would she do the same thing again?

It was a long time before she could give an honest answer to these questions, but through prayer and grace she has come at last to a state of sincere penitence. The impasse to God at last removed, her health, both spiritual and physical, has been restored. Today she is a transformed person. (H63)

Guilt

In thinking of guilt I consider the need to be sensitive to all with whom we come in contact, but most especially within the context of the healing ministry, where so many are vulnerable and can be badly, however inadvertently, harmed.

I recall all too clearly something that happened several months ago, and feel the same sense of outrage I experienced at the time. I saw in two very badly damaged individuals, once again, the devastation, physical, emotional, and spiritual, that can be wrought by guilt. In the case of this man and this woman, it was guilt inexcusably engendered during a healing ministry two years before.

The man had been told that his illness was punishment for his sin, a cruel, untrue, and unscriptural assertion. It had caused two years of needless suffering. Obviously he had overreacted, manifesting the extreme vulnerability of the sick. He knew with his mind that God would forgive no matter what the sin, but it frequently happens that the heart's cognition of God's forgiveness depends upon a human intermediary. I could not give him absolution, but I could and did give assurance of pardon. I prayed that his heart might be opened in the name of Jesus, and by the power of the Spirit, that he might be enabled to receive the forgiveness of God. That day he was healed of his guilt, and his shining face was an inspiration to me. At the final healing service, he was healed of his physical disability, which, incidentally, had caused him far less pain than the guilt.

As to the woman, wife of a Protestant minister, she came to me, pouring out her story of guilt and misery. She had had both breasts removed some years before, and had asked for prayer that the fear of recurrent cancer might be taken from her. Instead she was told that the breast cancer had been caused by a poor relationship with her mother and the many resentments she nourished. Until her relationship with her mother improved (particularly traumatic, as her mother, with whom she had a very good relationship, had recently died) and until she got rid of the resentments in other areas of her life, the cancer, she was told, most certainly would recur. This story seemed to me so unbelievable that I asked her husband to confirm it; he did.

I talked for a long time with this tormented woman and have rarely seen anyone so free of resentment. (I was the resentful one at this point—over her treatment!) For two years she had driven herself to the brink of breakdown, trying to find what wasn't there. Again, an overreaction, and for the same reason, and also an example of how the self-probing process can be overdone, degenerating into scrupulosity (spiritual nitpicking). This is why I advise people to spend no more than three or four minutes in daily self-examination, lest they become morbidly introspective, precisely what had happened to this poor woman.

How do we examine ourselves? There are many ways; none of them is all-sufficient, but any one of them can serve as a springboard. I often begin by checking myself either by reading the "fruits of the Spirit" (Gal. 5:22-23) or the Beatitudes (Matt. 5:3-11). Both of these are affirmative approaches, emphasizing the joy of the faith and the blessedness of our condition as Christians. Both can be easily adapted for self-examination. (S105)

Modes of confession
Every branch of the church provides some means of

confession, whether it be private confession, as in the Roman Catholic Church, or the corporate general confession provided by every Protestant denomination within the framework of its own particular service.

The nature of the corporate confession, as it is a general statement of our sinfulness rather than an explicit accounting of our faults, tends to make us gloss over any specific wrongdoings. The end of our general confession is likely to leave us as uncertain of God's forgiveness as we are indefinite about our sins. It is the explicit defining of our faults that gives them substance and enables us to know the reality of absolution.

But the love and mercy of God are obviously not restricted to those who partake of a sacramental rite. Saint John assures us, "If we confess our sins, he is faithful and just to forgive us our sins, and to cleanse us from all unrighteousness" (1 John 1:9). The only thing that really matters is that we ask, with sincerity and humility, the forgiveness of Jesus, secure in the knowledge that he will absolve us. (R136)

To say, "Lord, I'm sorry. Please forgive me," is all God requires. However, I have observed that, for various psychological reasons, it is not always enough for us.

Recently, I saw a good Christian man with a disfiguring skin condition healed by sacramental confession before we got to the laying on of hands. In that case, as in others, the requirement for that form of confession was not God's; it was the man's own need. Verbalizing his sins actualized his shame and sorrow. He had to shed his pride—a costly discipline which, by its very difficulty, was in itself a kind of expiation. Christians are called to share and to bear one another's burdens

(Gal. 6:2). That man needed someone to share his burden of guilt. My presence, as a Christian, emphasized that the penitent was a member of Christ's body and assured him of the spiritual support of the brethren whom I represented.

For these reasons the ancient church practiced open confession, in which the penitent confessed before the whole congregation. When the expansion of the church made this practice both impractical and dangerous for the penitent, private sacramental confession was instituted. A priest, representing the whole church, secretly heard confessions and granted absolution in the name of the Trinity. It was not then, nor is it now, a question of the priest's mediating between the penitent and God, for it is God's forgiveness that is sought by the penitent, and God who forgives. The absolution of the priest simply conveys God's forgiveness, just as the confession of the penitent makes contrition real.

Realizing that the corporate confession of their churches is neither intended nor sufficient for the confession of personal sins, and discovering that the daily self-examination, although invaluable, does not always suffice, an increasing number of Christians are unburdening their souls to someone they can trust, often a partner in prayer. The members of some small groups, following in the Wesleyan tradition, make an open confession when they feel the need. While the benefits of this custom can be great, so can its dangers, as the Wesleyan movement, and the ancient church before it, learned.

I believe in the sacrament of penance. I know it personally as a powerful means of grace, and I see it as a way to meet without danger the need for open confession. When confessing one to another fails because the authority of the church to give absolution is lacking, the sacrament of forgiveness succeeds.

A troubled woman came to see me a year ago. For some reason I was sure she needed to make a sacramental confession. She rebelled. "I didn't even know we had such a thing in my church," she said, and added wrathfully, "That's Roman Catholic, and I don't want any part of it!" I did not try to coerce her, but I pointed out that the custom of sacramental confession had begun, apparently, in the third century. Great leaders of the Reformation like Calvin, Luther, and Knox approved of this kind of confession and probably meant for their churches to retain it.

Two weeks later that woman made a life confession. Afterwards, her face flooded with joy, she said, "I never felt so wonderful and free in my life!" Her sins had been remitted; it was God's absolution, made actual, that enabled her to receive his forgiveness. (S94)

Accepting our forgiveness

The only danger in the Christian's concern with sin lies in the possibility that we cannot wholly accept the forgiveness of God. It is true that our Lord cautions us, "If ye forgive not men their trespasses, neither will your Father forgive your trespasses" (Matt. 6:15); and time after time we see this truth demonstrated in the healing ministry. A woman is at last able to forgive her husband's infidelity, and God's saving power flows unrestricted through her disease-ridden body, bringing healing in its wake. A man, deaf for twenty years, finally forgives the malice of his son, and through the redeeming power of God, his hearing is restored. And yet there are times when it seems more difficult to receive forgiveness than to give it. (H70)

The majority of disturbed people voice a common complaint and share a common problem: They are beset by feelings of guilt, and they are unable to accept the forgiveness of God. I have come to believe that this inability often has one primary source: lack of conviction that God really loves us. No matter how great the sin that may torture our conscience, no sinner is beyond the love of God. (S135)

Love

If *faith* evokes the power of God in our lives, and *repentance* releases it, it is *love* that ultimately fulfills it.

Wherever I have seen the healing ministry at work, I have observed the limitless power of love in action. Through today's manifestation of the Holy Spirit, many of us worship for the first time what we know to be the living God. We no longer have to struggle to love a disembodied Spirit or an Infinite Mind. We know God now as revealed in the gospels, through our knowledge of the living Christ. As our love meets the love of God, from which all love derives, miracles are wrought.

Time and again, in telling me of their healings, people have said in surprise: "You know, I wasn't even thinking of myself. I was praying for the person next to me, when I was healed." Typical is the experience of a middle-aged woman who had suffered a serious heart condition. "As I knelt at the altar," she said, "I could see that the woman next to me was in obvious pain. I was so anxious that she be healed that I forgot to pray for myself and prayed for her instead. While I was praying, I felt such peace and joy flood my entire being as surpasses description. I found myself almost running home and suddenly realized that I wasn't short of breath." A few days later this woman had another X-ray and cardiogram. She had been healed.

When I mentioned healings of this sort to a clergyman with a great deal of healing experience, he commented: "We know that an atmosphere of human love does reflect God's love. That's why when I lay on hands or administer unction, I like to have other loving members of the family present to pray with me. I have seen patients literally loved back to life."

If we were searching for the single attribute most characteristic of the healing ministry, I suspect we would find that it is *love*. This is not to imply that Christian love is restricted to the ministry of healing, but only to affirm that love is present to an unusual degree in people who are involved in any way with this ministry, whether they actively work in it, participate regularly in healing services as supplicants, or just believe in the healing of Christ.

We must first receive love in order to be able to give it. Love that does not express the love of God is an ineffectual thing. Against the backdrop and within the context of God's love for us, we can see others in a totally different way: in the light of the love of God for all his creatures. Through the healing ministry arises a chance to share with all humanity and to do more than share. It is not altruism, but rather a personal identification, a previously unknown empathy with those who suffer, and a creative sensitivity to the needs of others. (S45)

Agapic love

God's love is mirrored in human love and reflected in human action. But there is another kind of love with which I have become very familiar and which is a supernatural gift of God. As the healing ministry has illumined for me the entire faith and all the ministries of the church, so through it have I received my first insights into agapic love. This is an emotion entirely different from anything I have ever felt—one it seems to me impossible to define, for we have no words with which to work and no other emotion with which to compare it. It is not love in the ordinary sense, or pity, or compassion, or charity as we understand it; it is all these things but transcends them all. It is something outside ourselves with which we have nothing to do. Something of and from God surges up and overwhelms and quite literally stops us in our tracks with its power and the wonder of it. (M199)

The first time I became cognizant of it was several years ago when I walked into a sickroom. It was an ordinary room, inhabited at the moment by the patient, his wife, and a priest who was preparing to administer Holy Communion before the laying-on of hands.

Suddenly, as we knelt in prayer, that room was so powerfully transformed that it defies description. Our love, one for the other, seemed a palpable, visible thing. None of us had ever seen the other before, and most probably would never meet again. Yet each one of us, for those wonderful moments, would have given our life for the other; and as God's transcendent love washed over and into us, each would have fought for the privilege just then of being crucified for Christ. No evil of any sort, no sickness of any kind, could have withstood the power of this overwhelming and transfiguring force. A marvelous healing took place that day. (H48)

Emily was leading a mission at a church whose rector seemed cold and withdrawn. Moreover, the evening services were overlong and fatiguing because of a shortage of clergy to administer the healing rites. At the end of the service on the second night (which had been especially long and strenuous), she was greeting the people when a voice called out, "Mrs. Neal, come quickly! Someone has been hurt!" Outside in the snow lay a young man who had fallen, his crutches beside him. Here she describes the scene.

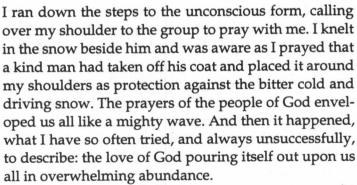

I ran down the steps to the unconscious form, calling over my shoulder to the group to pray with me. I knelt in the snow beside him and was aware as I prayed that a kind man had taken off his coat and placed it around my shoulders as protection against the bitter cold and driving snow. The prayers of the people of God enveloped us all like a mighty wave. And then it happened, what I have so often tried, and always unsuccessfully, to describe: the love of God pouring itself out upon us all in overwhelming abundance.

The young man stirred, opened his eyes, and sat up. Throwing his arms around me, he said, "Thanks." He then walked off into the night, leaving his crutches in the snow. As I walked back into the church, a chorus of voices spoke, "Now I know what you meant when you spoke this morning. I've never had an experience of the love of God like this."

On the final night of the mission, there were still only three of us to lay on hands. In the sacristy before the service started, all three of us prayed virtually the same prayer, "Lord, you know I've never been so tired in my whole life. Hold me up, please, and work through me, however exhausted I am." God never fails to answer this prayer, for his strength is indeed made perfect in our weakness. It then is that we live and work in the power of Christ, knowing that we of ourselves have no power. And so it was on that last night.

After the service, finally getting back to the sacristy, I found the two priests, their arms around each other's shoulders, and their eyes teary. They opened their arms to me, and we stood embracing, enfolded in God's love. We praised God mightily for all we had experienced. The rector, transformed into a warm, outgoing human being, said that people in the church who had not spoken to one another since he had come were now hugging each other. That whole church was healed through the great ministry of reconciliation, and God was beautifully and abundantly manifest. (T104)

The Sacramental Healing Rites

God's healing power is not limited to any one church, nor is its channeling confined to any one method. However, today's healing church has discovered the tremendous effectiveness of the sacramental healing rites used in the early post-apostolic church: the laying-on of hands and holy unction.

Not long ago a member of a non-sacramental church who was unfamiliar with the healing ministry asked whether I thought there was actual healing power in the rites themselves. My answer was, of course, "No." They are not black magic or a church-instigated form of sorcery. Of themselves, the sacraments have no weird healing properties. Essentially, they serve as channels through which God's healing power may flow. They are the means by which we can more easily receive a power infinitely greater than ourselves. As outward and visible signs of God's healing grace, they are an invaluable psychological aid in inspiring faith and arousing hope. For those too weak to pray, they are of incalculable comfort.

A woman who had suffered from a medically diagnosed abdominal cancer recalls: "I couldn't concentrate on prayer, and the effort of summoning up an active faith was just too much. All I could do was receive. When my minister laid on hands, I could virtually feel God's healing peace flow through my body. The pain left, and I fell into a natural sleep within minutes."

This patient was operated on the following day. Although there were clearly discernible evidences of the ravages of cancer, no trace of the malignancy was found. She is today in perfect health.

For those whose conscious minds cannot be reached, such as the insane, the unconscious, and young infants, the healing sacraments have again and again proved of inestimable value. I saw a clergyman anoint an infant reportedly dying from collapsed lungs. The baby was deathly pale, and even with the help of oxygen was breathing laboriously. As the minister ended his prayer, the infant stirred. I watched the color creep slowly but unmistakably into her ashen cheeks. The shallow, rapid breathing perceptibly deepened and slowed. She made a complete and rapid recovery.

A minister was called to lay hands on a man in his fifties who had suffered a cerebral hemorrhage. The doctors had warned his family that he could not be expected to regain consciousness before he died. Before the clergyman had lifted his hands from the patient's head, the man opened his eyes, in full consciousness, and smiled. Except for a scarcely discernible dragging of his left leg, the patient's recovery has been complete.

Mere chance, you say, that these results should coincide with the administration of the healing rites? I used to think so, but I have seen too many such cases to write them off as mere coincidences.

So many healings of this sort raise the interesting question as to whether the healing sacraments serve always as mere symbols, mere psychological aids. But what of recoveries such as those involving a tiny baby or an unconscious man, neither of whom could comprehend the symbolism of sacraments?

Many theologians of all churches now agree that the sacraments appear to have actual healing power, not of themselves, but according to the attitude of the person who receives them. Here again, some sort of faith must be involved. Obviously patients like those just mentioned are incapable of believing anything at all with the conscious mind; but the faith of the church, or the clergy, or the attendant family, or friends can supply the belief necessary to convert a symbol into an active agent of transforming power.

As the handshake is the physical act by which friendship is expressed, the sacraments are the physical means by which God's power is conveyed.

These sacramental rites are not essential for healing. It is by simple faith that we reach God, and by earnest prayer that we receive his power in our lives. However, God is a respecter of conditions. Whatever your feeling concerning the actual power inherent in the sacramental acts, it is undeniable that for many they help immeasurably in providing the occasion for healing and seem to create peculiarly favorable conditions for the operation of the Holy Spirit.

Clergy of all denominations have noted the effectiveness of the Episcopal Church—a sacramental church—in the healing field and have eagerly studied her methods. They find them to be based on those of the primitive church, where healing of the body was considered as vital a church function as the forgiveness of sins. In recognition of the fact that the laying-on of hands and anointing are New Testament healing techniques, most non-liturgical churches have adopted these same sacramental rites with outstanding results.

Several ministers of non-ritualistic churches have expressed concern as to how their congregations, not raised in the sacramental tradition, would accept the sacramental healing methods. A glance at the backgrounds of those attending Episcopal healing services has reassured them. And both laity and clergy apparently have no difficulty in accepting the historical precedent of the sacraments. They recognize in them methods instituted by our Lord.

The laying-on of hands

Spiritual energy, like electric power, is released at a point of contact. The sacraments seem to serve as extraordinarily strong points of contact with God, through which divine energy is released in our lives. They make the connection that releases a spiritual light so bright that it may illuminate the soul of a mere by-stander who happens to be within its arc.

Take the case of a friend of mine, a newspaper reporter. Last year during Lent he attended a noon service at a downtown church, which, to his surprise, was followed immediately by a healing service.

"I didn't have to be back at my desk for another half hour," he said, "so out of curiosity I decided to stay to find out what this was all about.

"I had never heard of the laying-on of hands, and when those who sought healing either for themselves or others were invited up to the altar rail, I sneaked up to a front pew to see better how this peculiar thing worked. I watched out of the corner of my eye as the clergyman laid his hands on each head, saying a brief prayer.

"He was only halfway down the line when there suddenly rushed through me the strongest conviction I have ever known of the actual presence of God. This was so profound and exciting an experience that I was unable to return to work. I went home instead to tell my wife what had happened. Since then we've both joined a church for the first time in our lives."

Jesus Christ repeatedly laid on hands to heal. And he charged his disciples to do likewise, saying, "In my name shall they cast out devils. . . . they shall lay hands on the sick, and they shall recover" (Mark 16:17-18). As the hands of Jesus were the channels of divine healing power, so were the hands of the apostles (Acts 28:8), and so are the hands of our healing ministers today.

This rite has actually been in continuous use through the centuries as a means of conveying spiritual grace. Not only is it used in confirmation and ordination, but at every church service throughout the year. The outstretched hands of the minister who pronounces the benediction represent the imposition of hands, which in the early church was individually administered to each communicant at the close of the service.

Here Emily writes compellingly about the laying-on of hands as an act of obedience to Jesus, and gives us a charming illustration of its effectiveness.

A good pragmatic reason to lay on hands is to call to the attention of all people the fact that Christ's healing power is available today as when he walked the earth. The church offers a therapy that many do not even know exists. But the real reason is, of course, that we lay on hands because our Lord told us to do this, by precept and example, and that is sufficient reason for doing it. "Naive literalness," some may say. If so, it is a naiveté that has been arduously acquired and proved to be true.

I was asked to lay on hands and pray for an Anglican nun who had been bedridden for many months in the infirmary on the third floor of her convent. When I arrived, she was brought downstairs and placed on a straight chair in the center of the room, the other sisters kneeling in a circle around her. She received the laying-on of hands. When the healing prayer was completed, I knelt for a few moments within the circle of nuns at prayer to offer thanksgiving and praise for the healing we knew had already been accomplished.

As we got up from our knees, the patient got up from her chair. "Thanks be to God," she said in a clear voice. She shook my hand and, without more ado, marched erectly and without hesitation up the stairs. She immediately moved from the infirmary back to her cell. As far as I know, she has not been back in bed, except to sleep, since that day. Her healing was complete.

This holy woman knows much more of the true meaning of the Eucharist than most of us, and she received the sacrament daily. Furthermore, she was for months the beneficiary of intercessory prayer offered by the other sisters in the convent, all of whom know more about intercessory prayer than I shall ever learn. Yet she could not walk until she received the laying-on of hands. We all wonder at something like this, but only briefly, for we have learned at long last not to question, but to believe, to love, and to obey.

I saw the nun a year later. She walked sedately down the long staircase to greet me. We shook hands, and then, with a twinkle in her eyes, she said, "I have to walk down the stairs slowly to make a dignified entrance. But I can run up and down them when no one is looking!" Whereupon she turned and, habit flying, raced up the steps and back again as fast as she could go!

Today, the laying-on of hands is employed in the ministry of healing both as a means of conveying the grace of God to the supplicant and as a means of intercessory prayer. It is common practice to participate in this rite not only for oneself, but with special intention for someone else who is in need.

I remember last summer, when the minister whom I joined in a healing service expressed himself in no uncertain terms on the subject. "It's just ridiculous," he exploded, "to believe that anyone kneeling *here* can receive the laying-on of hands for his Uncle Ed in Wisconsin." My answer was that the laying-on of hands received in this way is simply a form of intercessory prayer. When we receive for another, we simply bring the individual before God, praying that healing power may be released and asking that we may be open channels for the love and grace of God in the lives of those for whom we pray.

"Oh," said the priest, "I didn't understand. If this is what you do, of course it's all right."

The laying-on of hands is assuredly not the only means by which healing occurs. Many persons have been healed through the sacraments; thousands have been healed through prayer alone; some have been healed by reading a book concerned with spiritual healing or watching a religious television program. However, Christ has commanded his church to heal and has given us the methods by which healing may be accomplished. When the church is obedient, we find her every ministry uniquely blessed. The whole church, guided and indwelt by the Holy Spirit, knows true renewal, manifested by a great resurgence of spiritual power. (S110)

Anointing
While the laying-on of hands is a sacramental act, it may be used by certain spiritually gifted lay persons for healing. Anointing, however, is in a slightly differ-

ent category. Not a sacrament in the sense of the two great sacraments of baptism and Holy Communion ordained by our Lord, anointing is, nevertheless, a sacramental rite of the church. St. James actually initiated the format of today's healing church when he said, "Is any sick among you? Let him call for the elders of the church; and let them pray over him, anointing him with oil in the name of the Lord" (James 5:14).

As a better understanding of spiritual healing has developed, and anointing is gradually losing its widespread connotation of death, more and more clergy are reverting to its use. A growing number of non-liturgical clergy report that they regularly use consecrated oil in their healing work. The Roman Catholic Church has reestablished the original meaning of the sacrament with outstanding results.

Some ministers use the rite interchangeably with the laying-on of hands, and others use it exclusively. However, most clergy with very large healing ministries attended by diverse denominations prefer to administer it only when requested. They think its meaning is not yet sufficiently well understood to attempt its use in large, mixed groups.

Both the laying-on of hands and anointing have proved to be enormously effective channels for the healing power of the Holy Spirit. However, a good many ministers report instances of healing that follow anointing, after the imposition of hands has apparently failed.

A man suffering from tuberculosis, for example, had sought healing for many months. While his condition did not worsen, and spiritually he seemed improved, there was no marked change in his physical condition.

He finally asked for unction and was anointed one morning at ten o'clock. That afternoon was the first in over a year that his temperature did not rise. It remained normal thereafter; his disease was declared arrested, and he returned to work in an unusually short time.

Another case was that of a woman whose gradually failing eyesight finally resulted in total blindness. Her doctors told her it was hopeless to expect any sort of cure. Believing in Christ's healing power, she received the laying-on of hands a number of times, with no apparent result. She was anointed at the altar, at her request. On her way home from the church, she suddenly regained her vision.

The following case history tells of an unusual circumstance in which anointing was performed long-distance and, in a sense, by proxy.

Very late one night I was awakened by the ringing of the phone. On the line was a priest whom I had met once during a mission in his area. In a voice so weak as to be nearly inaudible, he told me that he was alone on a camping trip in Northern Canada, many miles from civilization and thus from either priest or physician. At that moment he was hemorrhaging badly from a bleeding ulcer. Would I pray for him over the telephone? Before I could answer, he said, "Wait! I feel as if I'm going into shock. I have blessed oil with me. Can I anoint myself?"

I had not the remotest idea how to answer him. And then I heard myself say, "Get the oil and bring it back to the phone with you." In an instant he was back, and I said, "As I begin the sacramental formulary, I'll be spiritually anointing you. But you dip your thumb in the oil and anoint yourself as I pray, making the sign of the cross on your forehead."

I proceeded with the prayer: "I anoint you with oil in the Name of the Father, and of the Son, and of the Holy Spirit. As you are outwardly anointed with this holy oil, so may our heavenly Father grant you the inward anointing of the Holy Spirit. Of his great mercy, may he forgive you your sins, release you from suffering, and restore you to wholeness and strength. May he deliver you from all evil, preserve you in all goodness, and bring you to everlasting life; through Jesus Christ our Lord." We joined together in a firm *Amen* and hung up.

Later the priest called to report that the hemorrhaging had stopped almost immediately. Upon his return home, he had told his physician what had happened. The latter immediately ordered the appropriate tests, the results of which the priest had just learned and had called to tell me. The ulcer of some years' standing was now completely healed. The only thing wrong with him was a slight anemia.

As I prepared to go to Mass that morning, I pondered what had transpired. Did it mean we should go about freely anointing ourselves? No, that would be contrary to the instructions of Jesus and would violate the sacramental principle that is closely tied in with the functioning of the body of Christ as a body and not just one individual. To me, the lesson to be learned from this healing is that God honors our spiritual intention. I was with that priest with my entire spirit, and with my spirit, empowered by the Holy Spirit, he was anointed. Perhaps, I reflect, this episode could be likened to the making of a spiritual communion. This was holy unction by spiritual intent. Once again we have a demonstration of the goodness of God, who honored our use of one of the means of grace given the church. (T122)

CHAPTER THREE

Prayer

The Foundation for Healing

———◆———

Emily's third book is, in her words, "a more intensely personal witness than either of the other two." It deals with her experiences in a realm that shortly before had been alien to her. Feeling herself a neophyte in this "realm of the Spirit," she initially resisted the urgings of readers, colleagues, and friends to write more deeply on the subject of Christian healing. But she longed to convey to others what she was learning about God's work in human lives, and she wanted also to respond in depth to the many questions that her readers were asking. So in 1961 she undertook this third book, The Lord Is Our Healer.

———◆———

The Realm of the Spirit

Many people have asked me if my earlier concepts of spiritual healing have changed. The most accurate answer is probably to say that my *attitude* rather than my *concepts* has altered. Although I never cease to marvel at the manifestations of God's healing power; of seeing with my own eyes a tumor dissolve, or a compound fracture instantly healed, I have in a sense become accustomed to physical healings. That is to say that I have learned to expect them, so that although they always amaze me, they no longer take me by surprise. But I have never, and know now that I never shall, become in any way accustomed to the healings of the spirit I have witnessed. In them I see, more clearly than ever before, the incontrovertible evidence of the Holy Spirit at work; the undeniable proof that God lives.

Not long ago, I was privileged to witness, with my physical senses, a remarkable healing of the spirit. I was asked to visit a man suffering from an incurable disease whose doctor had predicted he could not live out the week. I found him in an oxygen tent, from which he was removed during my visit. Fortunately he had a clear understanding of the healing ministry and a great deal of faith and needed little preparatory explanation, for I dared talk with him for only a moment, his color was so bad and his pulse so weak.

I laid on hands and began to pray, and suddenly in the middle of the prayer there was such an awareness of the presence of Christ that I couldn't continue. I glanced at the patient and was awestruck at what met my eyes. It was as if I could visibly see the Holy Spirit "stir up," as Paul puts it, the gift of God, which is in each one of us. I could see the hand of God literally mold, before my eyes, this man's spirit.

I saw the tears begin to flow down his cheeks and watched the color slowly flood his face. This whole episode must have taken place in less than sixty seconds, yet it seemed a lifetime. I knelt by his bed, then took the patient's pulse. It was strong and steady. He turned to me with the most extraordinary look of radiance, and said very quietly: "Today I have known God." As he spoke there flashed through my mind the lovely words of John Donne: "I shall not live 'til I see God; and when I have seen Him, I shall never die."

Although a number of physicians have been startled and impressed by instances of physical healing, many are also deeply affected by witnessing a spiritual experience in their patients. This was true with the case of a desperately ill man whom I visited at his home. I happened to arrive at the exact same moment as the man's doctor, which at the moment seemed to me peculiarly bad timing, but it was to turn out otherwise.

When I was introduced to the physician, I could feel his hostility assault me. He stated briefly and antagonistically that he had heard of the healing ministry, but obviously any alleged healings must be either psychosomatic or due to original misdiagnosis. He proceeded to examine the patient, then during my visit with the sick man, he waited in another room. He returned to the sickroom, and about ten minutes later we left the house as we had come, together. As we shook hands in parting, he said: "Medically speaking, that man should live only a few weeks, yet I have never felt such a strange peace and joy in any human being as I felt in him just now. I must confess that I am more profoundly shaken than I like to admit. What is this thing he has, anyway?"

"God," was the only reply I could make.

Forms of Prayer

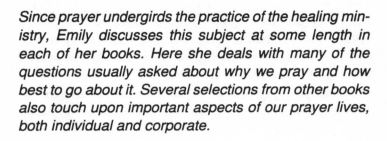

Since prayer undergirds the practice of the healing ministry, Emily discusses this subject at some length in each of her books. Here she deals with many of the questions usually asked about why we pray and how best to go about it. Several selections from other books also touch upon important aspects of our prayer lives, both individual and corporate.

Recently a woman asked a question I have heard voiced innumerable times, and not always by unbelievers.

"If God is all-knowing," she said, "why waste your time on prayer? Presumably you don't need to tell God the need. Besides, as long as he'll do what he wants anyway, what's the point of always saying, 'Let Thy will be done'?"

God gave many of us, myself included, inquiring minds—but if there is one thing I have learned over the past few years, it is this: There are certain areas in which strict obedience is required of us, and it matters not at all whether we understand or agree. Prayer is one of these areas. God works in our lives through prayer. We can't rationalize this, and we can't put ourselves in the position of arguing. It is an inviolable law which, if we want God's presence and power, we must obey.

We pray not to instruct or inform God, but as an act of faith that we may know better what he requires of us.

We pray, not in order to alter God's will, but to bring ourselves into accordance with it. We pray not necessarily to bring things to pass, but rather to bring the things of the kingdom into our cognizance. Obviously we can't change God—but through prayer God miraculously changes us.

Not long ago a man commented: "Prayer is certainly a wonderful thing. For years I have detested the man I work for. Circumstances got so bad a few months ago I decided in desperation to try praying and see if anything would happen. It certainly did. Today we are the best of friends. How God has changed him!"

What actually occurred here is that God changed the one who prayed. I have frequently had this same experience of disliking certain people; of finding certain circumstances almost unbearably difficult. When, as the result of prayer, my dislike has turned to genuine affection, and formerly untenable situations no longer seem bothersome, I have come to recognize that the change wrought by God is in me and my attitude—and not in the other person or the circumstances.

Not surprisingly, there is contained in the Lord's Prayer the elements of all prayer, including healing. "Thy kingdom come, Thy will be done, on earth as it is in heaven," might well serve as our basic prayer of faith, for in this single phrase is all we really need to know of healing prayer. It is the statement of our belief that the will of God is always for our good. When it is done on earth it means not calamity, as we seem invariably to expect whenever we say "Thy will be done," but the unspeakably wonderful things of God's kingdom, realized. When we change our attitude to recognize this, and to expect the best and not the worst, we will no longer pray fearfully, "Heal me, God, if it be Thy will," but confidently, "Heal me, God, according to Thy will that I should be well and strong and at peace." The difference here is infinitely more than the changing of one small word. It is the difference between an attitude of despair and one of victory.

When we first begin to pray, most of us do so with the intent of "using" God for our own ends. We proffer only a slightly different version of our childhood petition: "Please, God, don't let it rain tomorrow and spoil our picnic." But as through our prayer we grow closer to God, as we begin to understand that he has indeed "loved us with an everlasting love" (Jer. 31:3), then we strive perhaps for the first time to continue actively in God's love. It is then that our prayers change, and we begin to pray that God use us to his glory and not to our convenience.

"Never ask God to use you unless you really mean it," someone said to me once. I know now what he meant, for once you pray this prayer with your heart, God will take over your entire life, using you in ways and with a fullness that you cannot now even begin to imagine. A successful businessman, for example, gives up his career to work full-time in a witnessing prayer movement; a woman of great wealth dedicates her life to working with disadvantaged children; a brilliant physicist takes perpetual vows in a lay religious order; and so it has been with countless others.

The basic fundamentals of all prayer consist of the five so-called essential points: worship, thanksgiving, repentance, intercession, and petition. The inclusion of all these factors soon becomes instinctive in our every approach to God. As our prayer opens with adoration, we are inevitably led into thanksgiving for him whom we worship. As our hearts kneel before God, we are assailed by a sense of our own unworthiness and spontaneously we ask for absolution that we may remain in the Presence. Receiving it, we translate our gratitude into human terms and offer our prayers for others. Lastly, we petition God for our own needs, great or small.

Beyond these widely inclusive imperatives of prayer, I must believe that it does not matter whether we pray aloud or silently, or the exact words we say, or whether we use the words *Thee* or *You* when addressing God. What does matter above all else is the attitude of our hearts, for this alone determines the effectiveness of prayer, and in turn, the power we receive from God.

One meaning of the word *prayer*—a meaning with which too many of us have for too long been totally unfamiliar—is "joyous expectation": a joy often too deep for superficial gaiety but sometimes overflowing into tears; an expectancy that is not idle dreaming, but an abiding confidence in the validity of Jesus's promise. "Have faith in God," he said, "for whosoever shall say unto this mountain, Be thou removed, and be thou cast into the sea; and shall not doubt in his heart, but shall believe that those things which he saith shall come to pass; he shall have whatsoever he saith" (Mark 11:22-23).

These qualities of joy and expectancy, both born of faith, seem to me completely indispensable in any kind of prayer offered for any cause whatsoever. The fact that they are so seldom present, either singly or in combination, may well account for the fact that our prayers seem so often impotent.

Recently a woman said to me: "I guess my trouble is that I expect too much of God." Whatever her trouble may be, I know it is not that. None of us can ever expect too much of God. Our besetting sin, and I think it is a sin, is that we habitually expect so pitifully little, daring to impose upon God's mercy and power the limits of our own humanity.

As I believe we shouldn't be dogmatic about the words we say in prayer, neither, I think, should we be arbitrary about the way in which to pray. To me, for example, it seems important to pray as often as I can in the same place; to others, this doesn't matter at all. Many advisers on prayer advocate a relaxed and comfortable sitting position, especially for meditation; but I happen to prefer to pray on my knees, although I haven't always. Although Paul says, "On bended knee I pray the Father" (Eph. 3:14), I doubt that our physical posture makes much difference to God. Our spirits kneel in prayer regardless of the position of our bodies.

As I have learned to pray, for others as well as for myself, not for physical benefits alone, but for spiritual blessings, I have discovered that a curious phenomenon occurs. As in Holy Communion the material forms of bread and wine mystically become the spiritual food of the Body and Blood of Our Lord, so, conversely, are the spiritual blessings for which we pray mysteriously converted into the practical necessities for this earthly life.

To be granted a "mighty increase of strength by the Spirit," to know the "love of Christ which surpasses all knowledge," to be "filled with the entire fullness of God" (Eph. 3:16, 19) is the answer to our every need—the assurance of complete wholeness.

For me, then, these words become the foundation,

holding the key to the power of all petitionary and intercessory prayer—the prayer which we conclude with Paul: "Now to him who by the power at work within us is able to do far more abundantly than all that we ask or think, to him be glory in the church and in Christ Jesus to all generations, for ever and ever" (Eph. 3:20-21). This is the climax of our petition, in which we seek with confident expectation the fulfillment of all our needs, above all that we ask or even think, giving God the praise and the glory that this should be so.

All of us do not pray in the same way, but each of us who prays (whether we are taking our first tentative step toward God or whether we kneel, grateful beyond the telling, in God's presence) may be sure of one thing: "The Lord is nigh unto all that call upon him" (Ps. 145:18).

Listening, Reflecting, Meditating

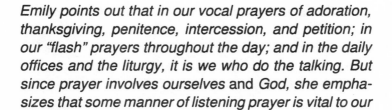

Emily points out that in our vocal prayers of adoration, thanksgiving, penitence, intercession, and petition; in our "flash" prayers throughout the day; and in the daily offices and the liturgy, it is we who do the talking. But since prayer involves ourselves and God, she emphasizes that some manner of listening prayer is vital to our spiritual welfare.

Only when we deliberately set our hearts in silence before God for a short time each day do we hear his voice, because then it is not drowned out by the strident cacophony of the world. In the noisy activism of our environment, that still, small voice needs the quietude of heart and mind if it is to be audible.

Many have remarked upon the difficulty of being quiet and just listening. Interior silence is difficult to achieve, and exterior silence frightens us. For the most part, we do not know how to handle it, let alone use it. Yet until we learn, deep prayer is impossible.

I think today with special gratitude of the great spiritual masters who have taught me so much of prayer and of the spiritual life: Saint Teresa of Avila, Saint John of the Cross, Saint Ignatius Loyola, Saint Francis of Assisi, Saint Augustine, Saint Thomas Aquinas, Saint Francis de Sales, the eighteenth-century Jesuit Jean Pierre de Caussade (the greatest spiritual director I have ever had), and all the rest. The core of their teaching is as relevant today as when they lived on earth.

Nevertheless (and paradoxically), the complicated structure of meditation so many of them taught in the Middle Ages proved to me a stumbling block for a long time. On paper, their individual methods of prayer first seemed highly complicated, but later, I learned to grasp the simplicity of these methods. It was years before I really comprehended Saint Teresa's metaphor of water used in describing her own stages of prayer or Saint John's "dark night of the soul." And the Ignatian exercises seemed to me impossibly rigid until I came to understand that his way of prayer was never meant to be inflexible.

For years the words *meditation* and *mental prayer* conjured up in my mind a system of intellectual gymnastics instead of that deep, quiet reflection that leads to the "conversation with Christ" of which Saint Teresa speaks. I finally learned to sift the wheat from the chaff (the latter of my own making), and came to learn the value of some structure in prayer, a structure that need not be complicated and must be adapted to the individual. We all have attractions to particular kinds of prayer. Sometimes these can be a trap, but they do keep us from attempting too soon a way of prayer that may seem difficult to us at first.

Yesterday a friend asked, "Where should I meditate? In a church?" If one can, a church is a good place, as interruptions are fewer than at home, and a church tends to be hallowed by prayers of the faithful. However, it is not necessary to pray always in a church. I remember how, long ago, imbued with the writings of the Desert Fathers, I created my own "desert" to which I could retreat. I learned then the value of praying in the same place every day.

In the beginning, my "desert" was my favorite chair in a corner of the living room. I found it helpful to set up a small table facing me, on which I placed a cross or a picture of Jesus. To close my eyes seemed to invite an onrush of distractions with which I could not cope. Focusing my eyes on a religious object helped me to concentrate. The distractions ("What shall I make for dinner tonight?" "Oh dear, it's raining. I wonder if the children remembered their umbrellas?") only poured in now; they did not rush! I learned not to fight them, for that gives them a force they should not have. I just tried to ignore them, and gently draw myself back to prayer. My prayer often seemed to consist largely of bringing myself back to prayer; in all honesty, there are still times when this is true.

When I finished my own meditation today, I recalled how a counselee had asked, "What should I meditate on?" I told her that a prerequisite of prayer is to immerse oneself in Scripture. My friend nodded and told me that she was reading the Bible straight through from Genesis through the Book of Revelation. This has never worked for me. Many of us seem to do better if we follow some daily reading plan. The Episcopal prayer book contains a daily lectionary, while the Roman Catholic missalettes contain daily readings. Further, there are a number of excellent Bible reading plans.

To follow such readings is to have daily material for meditation or, to use a less frightening word, *reflection*. Most spiritual directors suggest making one's meditation in the morning when one is fresh. My own experience has taught me that the time of meditation must depend upon the lifestyle of the individual. I do, however, suggest that the material for meditation be read the preceding night. Personally I have found it helpful to do this in bed shortly before going to sleep. The Scripture thus read seems to work on the unconscious mind during sleep, providing the yeast for prayer the following day.

The next day when it is time to pray, I advise silencing your telephone if you possibly can. Then retreat to your "desert." Before you actually begin to pray, prepare yourself as you will; I invariably ask for the guidance of the Holy Spirit. Since in prayer we offer our entire beings to God, I adapt the prayer of Ignatius for my own: "Take and receive, O Lord, my entire liberty, my memory, my understanding, my whole will. All that I am, all that I have, you have given me. I give it back again to you now, to be used according to your own good purpose." Then read slowly and thoughtfully the material selected and begin your meditation.

Keep in mind that the devotional use of the Bible is very different from study. To try to exegete the passage can be death to the spirit of prayer! You are in no hurry, and if the first sentence should "jump out" at you, stay with it for the entire time of the meditation if you so desire.

If you have chosen a Gospel passage, reflect upon what Jesus is saying to you. If you wish, make yourself part of, and a participant in, the scene depicted. However, you do not have to do this. The important thing to remember is the fundamental rule of prayer enunciated by Teresa, when she states that prayer consists not in thinking much but in loving much. To still one's mind, to talk little, and to listen hard—this constitutes a way of prayer that can lead to union with God.

Talk with our Lord about the material you have just read. This is a two-way conversation with God. Thus our prayer should be, "Speak, Lord"—and then, in silence, we listen. This colloquy with Jesus should be primarily an intimate union of friendship with him, at the same time never forgetting that he is God.

The conclusion of our prayer time consists of thanking God for what we have received. I like to end it all with the Our Father. I have found this general conclusion of prayer more satisfactory than the traditional "gathering up the fruits of our prayer" and making a definite resolution which we offer to God. For me, there often are no immediately discernible fruits. These are more apt to be cumulative. However, all of this is flexible, as is my personal custom of leaving five or ten minutes of the meditation time to write the conclusion of the prayer. These I call my "Letters to the Lord," and keep them in a notebook as part of a spiritual journal.

The Jesus prayer

If we should be immersed in Scripture in order to pray well, so also should we be saturated in Christ. One way to achieve the latter is to learn the use of the ancient Jesus prayer, "Lord Jesus Christ, Son of God, have mercy upon me, a sinner." This prayer reaches back to the New Testament, and has been used for centuries in monasteries and among the laity for meditation and contemplation, particularly in the Eastern Orthodox Church. However, curiously enough, at the time that I began to use it, I did not know this, for I knew nothing whatsoever about it except the words. But through the healing ministry I had learned of the power in the Name of Jesus.

For a reason I cannot explain other than to believe it to be the guidance of the Holy Spirit, I began to repeat the Jesus prayer at intervals during the day—at first just occasionally as I made the beds or dusted or prepared dinner. Then gradually, and scarcely realizing what I was doing, I began to repeat it more and more frequently, until it seemed to become a subconscious refrain undergirding my life and accompanying all I did. The more I used it the more aware I became of a remarkable thing: a constant underlying and sustaining spiritual current, which was a means of bringing me close to God and holding me continuously in God's presence in a way I had never before experienced or thought possible.

During a brief period, I stopped this prayer to see

what, if anything, would happen, wondering if my imagination were not getting the better of me. I felt at once an overwhelming lack, a sense of deep loss, curiously bereft, and strangely deprived. I returned to it gratefully and think now I could not live without it. Although far from proficient in this way of prayer, the more I have practiced it, the more I have grown in it.

Begin it with a few minutes a day, and slowly increase it; and as you do, you will find it gradually penetrating your subconscious to the point that your heart will be repeating the prayer wherever you are or whatever you are doing. The time will come surprisingly quickly when it will take no time, although it will occupy your life. There will be no interference with all the other activities of your existence, only an increased enlightenment and ability to perform your tasks; and a continuing sense of the presence of Christ that will fill you with a joy and wonder as unceasing as your prayer.

It will gently propel your life in a constant movement towards God, for it simultaneously springs from and permeates your innermost being, focusing every level of your mind and centering your entire heart and spirit in God.

This is a simple prayer, to be sure, but it can take you to the highest form of prayer there is, if you are so led. Perhaps because it contains the spirit and hence the power of all prayer, it is not only limitless in its scope, but infinite in its use. You can also use it on behalf of others and for the world: "Have mercy on us; have mercy on them."

In mentioning this prayer someone said to me; "But what about our Lord's words against 'vain repetitions'?" The answer to this is that the repetition in this prayer is not "vain."

Our Lord admonishes the Pharisee for hypocrisy expressed in meaningless words, not the repetition of the Name that evokes and expresses the faith in one's heart. In each repetition, the words may be the same but never twice identical, for their meaning is inexhaustible. Your intent and your emphases shift and change as you pray this prayer.

Begin the prayer in dryness, as a mechanical act of your mind—but with each repetition your heart and spirit yield, until the words become true prayer. Begin it in little faith—but Christ honors your obedience, and with each repetition your faith increases. Begin it in coldness—but your consecration and devotion grow each time you repeat the same Name, the same prayer said ten thousand times, yet never in the same way.

I cannot possibly explain the full power of the Jesus prayer. I only know that it has changed my life. (M131)

Intercession

Earlier, Emily touched upon intercession as one of the five basic subjects of prayer, which are sometimes called the five "points" or "fingers" of prayer. As the means by which we bring to God those who suffer brokenness, intercession is a major function of the healing ministry in both public and private settings. Here Emily describes some of her experiences in various aspects of intercessory prayer.

---◆---

Anyone who has ever been on the receiving end of intercessory prayer knows what it can mean. To be upheld in prayer is not merely a vaguely comforting thought; it is to receive a very real and tangible strength.

In traveling around the country I have acquired an unusually long prayer list, for wherever I go, people ask for prayer. But it works both ways, for a great many place me on their prayer lists, which means that hundreds of people, most of whom I don't know, are praying for me. No one but God knows how grateful I am that this is so, for I think we are all desperately in need of each other's prayers, and none of us can ever have enough—not only in times of particular crisis, but throughout our daily lives.

A thousand times I have felt the effects of these prayers at the most unlikely times. Often while walking down the street, or sitting in a theater, or shopping or preparing dinner, I have suddenly known that wonderful elevation of the spirit, that flooding with joy, that surge of vitality, which are the result of prayer. So undeniable is the impact, yet in the beginning so incredible did the whole thing seem to me, that I used to check back whenever possible. Time after time I would discover that at the precise time that I had experienced these reactions, someone was in prayer for me. No one knows better than I how absurd this sort of thing can sound—or how unbelievable, but again and again it happens.

On one day I felt so spiritually drained after long periods of prayer for a close relative, that I asked my rector to pray not only for the patient but also for me. The prayers concluded, I went back to work, and within minutes felt such a joyous soaring of my heart and such a sense of spiritual strength and fullness that I dropped my pencil and paused in momentary wonderment before I realized what it was.

Praying for strangers

Having myself so often received the benefits of intercessory prayer, I began some time ago, both as an experiment and in the hope of bringing comfort, to pray for strangers. This has been a fascinating venture, often evoking fantastic results.

In one instance I recall a particularly sullen and uncooperative taxi driver. Annoyed, I instinctively started to react in the same way—by being equally disagreeable. And then, more as a game than anything else, I said a short prayer for him. The change in his attitude was instantaneous. He became jovial and talkative, and as we entered the street of my destination, he turned off his meter with a block yet to go. As I got out of the cab I said: "God bless you the rest of the day." He grinned and replied: "He already has. I don't know why, but I suddenly feel wonderful!"

In the certain knowledge that prayer brings solace, it has become my custom to pray for the bereaved whenever a funeral procession passes; for the occupant of the ambulance that shrieks down the street; for the worried-looking woman in the supermarket; for the drunk staggering outside the bar; for the lame man a few houses down whom I don't know but often see laboriously walking up the hill. I believe that somehow these people will feel the power of prayer and be helped.

In reflecting on the remarkable efficacy of prayer I can only wonder that our churches do not utilize the tremendous prayer power that lies latent within them. In times of disaster, such as floods or hurricanes, airplane accidents or train wrecks, or any headlined catastrophic event, I could wish that every one of our churches would offer prayer on Sunday mornings for the survivors. We cannot compute the comfort, the strength, the peace that it might bring—and it would take such little time and effort to do.

Praying for loved ones

For those whose loved ones are ill, intercessory prayer is of vital importance—and it is well to pray not only for the patient's recovery, but also for the spiritual strength of the family, that they may prove better channels for God's healing power. No matter how strong one's faith, the closer we are to the one who is sick, the more difficult the situation tends to be. Our fear, however (which is almost inevitable), should never prevent our praying for those we love, for love is stronger than fear. Nor should we, I think, in our determination to pray the affirmative prayer of faith, feel guilty or ashamed if all we can at times muster is "Christ have mercy upon us."

The young son of a woman who firmly believed in the healing Christ was stricken with spinal meningitis. The medical prognosis was negative. Distraught and fearful, the mother called a friend experienced in prayer and asked her help. They agreed upon a certain hour at which time the friend would pray for healing, while the mother laid hands upon her son. This procedure was repeated three different times, and the child made a rapid and complete recovery. The doctor in charge called it a miracle.

The physical cures resulting from intercessory prayer are no more dynamic than the spiritual ones, but they are more outwardly dramatic, and the tangible results of prayer are more obvious in physical healing than in other areas. We are able to correlate the healing with the precise time of prayer, which gives us a clear indication of cause and effect.

From personal experience I know that we are greatly helped by prayer whether or not we know we are being prayed for. From observation, I know that even the unbeliever can receive healing through the prayers of the believer. But as a general rule, the patient should not only know (or if unconscious, a close relative should know) but cooperate if possible, by praying at the same time as the intercessory prayer is offered.

Whenever I receive the laying-on of hands on behalf of someone else, I ask that the patient be in prayer at the same time. Conversely, I have on my prayer list a number of people in other cities who attend healing services where they live. I am in prayer for them at home at the same hour that they are receiving the healing rites.

Many people who call me say apologetically: "I know you're busy, and I hate to ask anything more of you, but would you mind praying for so and so?"

Mind? It seems to me that to pray for others is the greatest privilege any of us can ever know. That through our prayers we may be instrumental in releasing the power of God in the lives of others gives a new and wonderful purpose to our lives. We receive far more than it lies in our power to give, for our praying for others increases our sensitivity and receptivity to prayer, which in turn brings us always closer to the God we worship.

In this passage from The Healing Ministry, *Emily emphasizes the need to prepare ourselves for intercession and offers a simple mode of visualization for use in intercessory prayer.*

In order that we may be effective instruments, the first step in intercession is to offer ourselves for preparation. Toward that end, we pray that the Holy Spirit may increase in us, strengthen our faith, and increase our love. We pray for the forgiveness of our sins, both known and unknown.

As sins such as resentment, jealousy, and envy impede the inflow of God's healing power, so may these same sins, if unconfessed, diminish the effectiveness of our prayer for others. I believe one of the most serious hindrances to efficacious prayer, whether for ourselves or others, lies in our failure to forgive those who have hurt us. So we pray that God may help us to forgive as he has already forgiven.

We praise God in whom we live and move and have our being. We offer God thanksgiving. And then we begin to intercede.

There are so many ways to do this. Among the simplest: We bring those for whom we pray, one by one and each by name, before God. Their hands in ours, standing together in the divine light, we give praise and thanksgiving for their lives, asking that they be made whole, all brokenness mended. Quietly and without harassment, we bring each soul to Jesus, resting with them in him, our only desire that he may be glorified.

I often pray something like this: "Blessed Lord Jesus, possess me who comes before you now as intercessor. In union with you, who lives to make intercession, I pray for N—. I pray for the healing of his entire person; I pray you will give him a trustful and serene mind." An attitude of trust and serenity tends to set free within those for whom we pray the power of the resurrected Christ.

We must beware always of the temptation to focus our attention on the brokenness for which we pray, rather than on Jesus who is even now touching those we bring before the throne of grace, healing and making whole each one. As in our mind's eye we see him stretching forth his hand to heal, we see the sick, the bereaved, the suffering from any cause, transformed into radiant and joyous persons as the result of his life-giving touch. (T99)

Prayer Groups

In union there is strength—and prayer is no exception. The prayer group movement, a lay movement, has spread all over the world. There is scarcely a country where there cannot be found small circles of men and women praying together.

The support of a prayer group can strengthen and enrich a church's worship, outreach, and other activities. I think it is no exaggeration to suggest that without the existence of such groups, there would be no healing ministry at all. For not only does a healing ministry without such prayer support inevitably seem to fail, but it is most often through the results of the prayers of the faithful that such a ministry is begun and empowered to proceed.

Take, for example, a church I visited two years ago. The pastor had not as yet instituted healing services, nor did he apparently have any plans for doing so in the immediate future. "My people aren't ready for it yet," he had told me the night before I spoke. "The truth is, I'm not sure that I know enough about it."

The next day after my address several women came to me and asked that I prevail upon their minister to begin healing services. I explained that this was not my affair, and suggested that if they really wanted such services, they should first form a prayer group with their pastor's consent.

Subsequently, five women of the parish arranged to meet weekly to study and to pray for the sick and for the establishment of a healing ministry in their church. Within a few months this group expanded to twelve, and the minister was so impressed with the spiritual power generated by the group that within the year he inaugurated a healing ministry.

If corporate prayer were to realize even a fraction of its potential, the course of history might well be altered. Through it, the power of God becomes a viable and unassailable force, frequently discernible by the unbeliever, who, no matter what he calls that power, responds. An agnostic psychologist, reluctantly present in a church where hundreds prayed in faith for the sick, remarked: "I'm not prepared to call what I feel here, *God*—but neither will I deny that a force of some kind is being released."

"Where two or three are gathered together in My Name, there am I in the midst of them," said our Lord, and anyone who has felt the power of corporate prayer knows how true this is. I have felt this power in a living room, where five people prayed together for the restoration of a broken marriage. I have felt it in a parish hall, where group prayer was offered for the mending of international relationships. I have felt it in a church, lit by the light of Christ, as many knelt in prayer for the recovery of a sick child. And most recently I felt it in a church in the Midwest where I had gone to speak.

When I arrived that afternoon, I was told that the Roman Catholic husband of the church's caretaker had suffered a severe coronary attack the previous day. The medical prognosis was negative, and he had received the last rites of his church at noon.

My audience that night was predominantly men, including a number of doctors, of whom several were thought to be antagonistic to the healing ministry. Unusually sensitive to any hostility in an audience, I felt none that night either during the address or the question period which followed. Throughout, the presence of God was so unmistakable, that as one man afterwards graphically expressed it: "If a dog had wandered in here tonight, his hackles would have risen."

At the conclusion of the program, the minister began the benediction—then abruptly halted, and visibly moved, said: "I feel so much power here I feel impelled to ask your prayers for someone who is dying." He told briefly of the patient's heart attack; the audience rose to its feet, and he proceeded to lead them in prayer for the sick man. The sense of the Presence seemed to increase, and as the prayers ended, the power seemed a palpable thing.

A week later, I received a letter from the clergyman: "The night we prayed, the patient was awake and himself in prayer as he looked at the crucifix on the wall of his hospital room. He suddenly became aware of the presence of a second person in the room and heard the words: 'You will live, and you are saved by prayer. But not your own.'"

How any particular healing group functions must be determined by the desire of its members and the environment surrounding them. In many churches, a good proportion of the prayer group attends each service. The presence and prayers of expectant believers spiritually strengthen those officiating and are of great benefit to those at the service with a less developed faith who are seeking healing. In some churches it is customary, when there is a special and urgent need, to notify the prayer band, which then attends the service en masse, receiving the laying-on of hands for the critically ill person.

Those doctors who are familiar with the healing ministry and therefore sympathetic to it ask the cooperation of prayer groups. When a patient is seriously ill, the doctor asks for intercessory prayer, and in some instances requests members of the prayer group to pray at the bedside of a patient. Not long ago, for example, a teenage boy involved in an automobile accident lay crushed and apparently dying in a large city hospital. Four members of a prayer group were called, and prayed together at his bedside. The boy recovered to the astonishment of all but one doctor—the one who had contacted the prayer group—who said, "When you made your prognosis, you forgot to take into account the power of prayer."

Generally it is good for a prayer group to include members of different churches. As one Episcopalian observed: "For several years we have struggled along with a purely Episcopal group. A few months ago we included a Baptist, a Methodist, and a Presbyterian, and we have assumed a new vitality, with startling evidence of the healing Christ." Perhaps this is because we have in these mixed groups an approximation, however infinitesimal, of the power of the church universal.

I recently heard a minister refer to prayer-group work as a "vocation," and I recalled the words of Saint Paul: "I therefore beseech you that ye walk worthy of the vocation wherewith ye are called" (Eph. 4:1).

In order to "walk worthy," I believe there must be a proper balance struck between prayer groups and the sacramental life of the church. We all need the stabilizing influence of the church if we are to avert those dangers inherent in any religious work—the danger of pride. We have to be aware of the danger of feeling ourselves members of the spiritual elite, who alone know "how" to pray; the danger of spiritual arrogance, which is surely greater than any other arrogance on earth except that of ignorance; the danger of an ostentatious religiosity, which more often repels than converts. I believe a group must feel responsibility, but never self-esteem, for nothing accomplished through intercessory prayer is done by any human being or in any way involves personal merit.

We do not fully understand the power of corporate prayer, or why receiving the laying-on of hands on behalf of others is effective, or why the person for whom intercessory prayer is offered should pray simultaneously. We only know that experience has proved again and again that these things do have importance.

We also know that through the fellowship of the concerned, who believe God loves and cares, Christ's healing light is released upon a sick and suffering world. These groups of devout men and women are quietly and unobtrusively demonstrating Christ's promised power.

Practicing God's Presence

———————◆———————

Having considered the basics of private prayer and intercession, and the need for prayer in small groups, Emily emphasizes that where any prayer group grows in spiritual strength, it is because each member seeks a closer personal relationship with God. Bringing us back to private prayer, she describes here a more advanced discipline known as practicing the Presence.

When a friend told her, in some consternation, that she had never felt God's presence and wondered whether all of us are meant to know it, Emily replied, "I believe that anyone who wants God enough can know his presence." In what follows she discusses the daily, even hourly, recollection needed in practicing God's presence, some of the dangers of excess, and how to deal with feelings of separation from God that confront most Christians at some point along their way.

———————◆———————

As the existence of God does not depend upon our acknowledgment of it, so the actuality of God's presence does not depend upon our recognition. Wherever we are, and under whatever circumstances, each of us is continually surrounded by God whether or not we are actively aware of it. Nevertheless, it is an indisputable fact that God's love and healing power become available to us in direct accordance with our conscious identity with him and our confession of the reality of the living God.

For many of us, to cultivate our awareness, so that we may know when we stand in God's presence, takes considerable time and practice on our part. As there is more than one road to faith, as there is more than one way to pray, so is there more than one way of practicing the presence of God. I can only tell you how it has been with me.

It was a long time after I had intellectually accepted the premise that God continually surrounds and pervades each one of us, that I actually knew the Presence and recognized it as such. It began one night as I prayed during my husband's illness. For the first few days after his return from the hospital, I was able to pray fairly confidently, but it soon became obvious that I wasn't as confident as I had thought. As the days went by and the nervous strain accumulated, my prayers gradually deteriorated into an incessant and powerless repetition, "Please God heal him—Please God heal him." Then one night I was too tired to pray at all except, "Lord have mercy. I believe, help thou mine unbelief."

Suddenly the profound longing for my husband's physical healing was replaced by what I can only describe as an overwhelming spiritual thirst. Simultaneously there washed over me a feeling, not at all of resignation, but of indescribable peace. At that moment there was a sudden instantaneous flash of awareness that went as quickly as it had come—so quickly, indeed, that time-wise, the experience might well have been a product of wishful thinking. Yet the impact was so tremendous and so lasting, that were I never to have had that experience again, I think I could not for the remainder of my life have denied that it actually happened.

Many months went by before a repetition of this experience, and it was during those months that, for the first time, I began to meditate as well as pray: to become absolutely still and abide in the love of God. This was the period in which I learned to contemplate God in all of his majesty and mercy, and to meditate each day on some of Christ's words:

> "He that loseth his life for my sake shall find it" (Matt. 10:39).

> "If any one thirst, let him come to me and drink" (John 7:37).

> "I am the way, the truth, and the life" (John 14:6).

This was the period in which the words, "Be still and know that I am God," became more than just a phrase from Psalm 46. It was in this silence that I learned to listen to God.

There are some who tend to use meditative prayer almost exclusively, but for most people, as for me, a combination of meditation and prayer has proved the best answer—the most effective means of realizing the Presence. It is as if through prayer we reach out to touch the hem of God's garment, while by meditation we are enveloped in it. The reaching out is as vital as the enfoldment; each is dependent on the other.

This is part, although only a part, of the practice of the Presence, by which means that initial flash of awareness may be repeated and gradually sustained over longer periods of time.

A twenty-four hour effort

I soon learned that the practice of the Presence could not be confined to an hour or so of prayer and meditation a day, but is actually a twenty-four-hour-a-day proposition. It means offering yourself to God when you get up in the morning, and giving yourself to God when you go to sleep at night. It means acknowledging God's continued presence by the frequent saying of little prayers of praise and thanksgiving, however short, as you make the beds or ride to the office. Even a silent repetition of the name of Jesus will suffice.

In the beginning, you will do these things self-consciously, in hope. Then you will do them by rote, alternately thinking the whole thing pretty silly or a lot of superstitious nonsense. For a long time you may seem as far from your goal as when you started. And then, one day, you will know God's presence.

The means by which you have for so long laboriously tried to cultivate an awareness of God—the meditating you have done, the prayers you have said—will no longer seem meaningless. They will have become for you a way of life, and suddenly you won't know how to live any other way. You will recognize God's hand in everything you do and everything that happens in your life. And, curiously, you will discover that the more you consciously acknowledge and recognize the hand of God in your life, the more frequently it will actually be upon you in mercy and compassion.

"Draw nigh to God, and he will draw nigh to you" (James 4:8). These words will become for you a demonstrable truth, as more and more often you will feel the Presence and will be able to remain in it for increasingly long periods of time. But in that lies a hazard against which we must continually be on guard.

The danger of excess

To know the Presence is to know God in a special and wonderful way. Once having stepped into the Presence, you will want always to be in it. You won't be alone in your emotional response, but it is something of which to be careful, for if your desire becomes too great, it can be dangerous and lead to serious emotional unbalance. Spiritual gluttony is as harmful as any other kind. While I believe that we can't want God too much, I also believe that we can want too much of God, with the result that we may be tempted to withdraw from the rest of the world.

This is the sort of attitude we must at all costs avoid, for it degrades our dedication to Christ into a neurotic religiosity contrary to his will. From the beginning, God has worked through human beings, and Christianity is a faith relevant to, and (for the vast majority of us) best demonstrated in, the world at large. Jesus commands us to love God with all our hearts, but also to love our neighbors. He never said to withdraw from them that we might worship God the better.

By the power of the Holy Spirit through prayer and worship, our individual spiritual batteries are recharged—but unless we reach out to others, we hide our light under a bushel. God cannot be glorified in the darkness.

To attempt to offer ourselves to God as solitary and attenuated spiritual beings is both futile and unrealistic, for even at best, this will not result in sinlessness, but only in the mutilation of our humanity. It is in letting God shine through, direct, and hallow our everyday work, whatever it is, that we may bear the most telling witness. In trying to separate ourselves from humanity, we are, however unintentionally, separating ourselves from God and thus inadvertently removing ourselves from sanctifying grace.

It may seem that I unnecessarily stress the danger of what, after all, does not seem a too-prevalent hazard in our culture: an excess of spiritual zeal. I freely acknowledge that this tendency does not pose a problem in most areas of the faith, where the problem is likely to be just the reverse. However, unlike some critics of the healing ministry who fear that concern with the physical may take precedence over the spiritual, I believe that in the healing field there is most frequently an overemphasis of the spiritual. This is not due to fanaticism, but rather to the fact that this ministry is so peculiarly pervaded by the presence of Christ, and those who are continually surrounded by the evidence of his love and mercy can easily develop a reluctance to step out of the light into the comparative darkness of the world at large.

Many of us need reminding from time to time that as

Christians we must live always in two worlds simultaneously, the spiritual and the physical. It is imperative that a sane balance between the two be struck and maintained. To emphasize one at the expense of the other must inevitably result in a maimed personality, both nullifying the meaning and negating the lesson of the Incarnation.

Having known the Presence, if only once and only for an instant, you will always remember how it was. Neither your heart nor your mind will ever again be restless in the old way. You will have found peace. And yet, in one tiny corner of your being, there will reside for as long as you live a yearning that cannot be entirely satisfied in this life.

Spiritual dryness

I have spoken of cultivating an awareness of the presence of God and cautioned against the possibility of going overboard by seeking spirituality to the exclusion of other things God may wish for us. But another factor equally relevant to our conscious contact with God concerns the apparent loss of that contact after it has been established.

Occasional periods of spiritual dryness are a common occurrence with anyone who prays. Most of us have known many times when our prayers seem to be discouragingly laborious and barren. But I was totally unprepared for the first extended period of profound and devastating spiritual desolation that suddenly assailed me for no apparent reason some time ago. This was no mere "dryness." It was a terrifying sense of irrevocable separation from God. Believing that only unrepented sin can separate us from God, I racked my brain and conscience for days to no avail in an effort to unearth some sin.

Although living a full and ostensibly normal life, surrounded by family and friends, I was actually existing for what then seemed an eternity of time in the greatest sense of aloneness I have ever known. If this was a sign of spiritual development, I had only one desire: to remain always a pygmy!

As time went on, my disposition grew worse. I became nervous and irritable—the inevitable outgrowth of a profound disorientation—and at the same time felt increasingly upset that this was so, realizing that my reaction of itself was creating an impediment to God's love, and thus jeopardizing any hope of a quick reconciliation.

Day after day, I continued to pray (for by this time prayer had become a deeply ingrained habit, and I no longer knew how to live without it). At first I pleaded for just one more moment's awareness of God. I felt, in a very real sense, as if I were dying of thirst, a thirst no substance on earth could relieve. And then one day as I prayed, there seemed wrung from my innermost being the silent cry, "Jesus, hear me," and simultaneously there flashed through my mind the words I didn't even know I knew: "He liveth to make intercession for you" (Heb. 7:25). And suddenly Christ was there.

Much of the joy of this reconciliation was clouded by my subsequent inability to rest and relax in God. For weeks I lived in dread of a repetition of this experience—but as time went on I regained my equilibrium and could make a fairly painless effort to fathom what had caused it all. I suspect that these periods of spiritual desolation, in which the so-called "consolations" or tangible rewards of prayer are withheld, can be due to any one of a number of reasons or a combination of several.

Perhaps they are caused by an unconscious spiritual pride on our parts, because of what may have seemed the former effectiveness of our prayers; or perhaps it is simply spiritual exhaustion that is responsible. Perhaps they are the result of our spiritual gluttony—an insatiable appetite for more than we are meant to have—or perhaps they are due to the intervention of the devil, who, the closer we come to God, works more assiduously to destroy the relationship.

I think it can never be a question of God deliberately withdrawing from us as a punishment. "I will never leave thee, nor forsake thee" (Heb. 13:5) is God's promise—the promise on which our faith stands. God is always there, steadfast, unchanging, and merciful. The veil of separation is never over God's face, but only over ours.

I have learned much of the spiritual value of these experiences of dryness, for my first one was not to be the last, although never since the first time have I suffered the same sense of panic and devastation. I am able to relax now in the inestimable comfort of the believing knowledge that Christ is indeed continually making intercession; and I rest now in my heart's cognizance, as well as in my mind's conviction, that his promise, "Lo, I am with you alway, even unto the end of the world" (Matt. 28:20), has never been withdrawn.

CHAPTER FOUR

The Ministry of Death

———◆———

In 1961, just a few years after her discovery of the ministry of healing, Emily's life was shaken by the illness and death of her husband of thirty-one years, Alvin Neal. Her fourth book, In the Midst of Life, *deals not only with this death and its effects on her life and ministry, but also with the meaning of death as it touches the lives of all Christian people. Breaking through her natural reserve in intensely personal matters, Emily here opens her heart to her readers, sharing with us her inmost thoughts, her regrets, her struggles, and her joys.*

In this chapter she gives advice to the bereaved, and to those who minister to the bereaved—as friends, as pastors, and as the corporate body of Christ. From the experiences recorded here there emerges a solid base from which the church and her people can undertake what Emily calls "the ministry of death," which is, she says, "in its fullest sense, a healing ministry."

———◆———

A Great Paradox

Spiritual healing, like all Christian faith, is filled with paradoxes; and one of the greatest of these lies in the fact that while the ministry of healing emphasizes complete wholeness—healing of the body and mind as well as the spirit—yet it has proved time without number to be the finest preparation and greatest comfort in time of death.

Recently I have been most intimately associated with the case of a woman who for the past several years has devoted her life to the furtherance of the healing ministry. Nevertheless, despite the thousands of prayers offered for her husband, and the ministrations of the healing church, he died a few months ago at the age of fifty-three. I know this woman and her reactions well, for I am she.

My spiritual life has been more profoundly changed by the experience of my husband, Alvin's, death than by anything except my initial discovery and acknowledgement of the living God. It has been, in a very real sense, a second conversion, and in a curious way more powerful and certainly more dramatic than the first, which was a slow and difficult growing into faith.

After Alvin died I was to understand what *the communion of saints* really means, the ineffable comfort it could truly bring the bereaved. But this article of faith is far more than a tenet of comfort. For us, the living, it provides the spiritually demonstrable evidence of the validity of the Christian promise that there is no death.

Believing that our dead live in Christ, we make an unspeakably wonderful discovery through the communion of saints: We find that they have not really died to us in terms of love or help, influence or spiritual presence.

In connection with this, I think often of a fairly typical experience of World War II, and liken it to what has happened now. Alvin was a naval officer, and early in the war our family was all together in San Diego for several months. Without warning he was transferred to the East Coast, and the children and I were to remain in California until we heard from him. At last the call came: He was on an aircraft carrier operating out of Quonset, Rhode Island. Within five miles of the base was a delightful New England village which he knew we would love, so he asked us to come East as soon as we could get train reservations. Within a week we were off, and arrived in Wickford, Rhode Island, early in March—the only living accommodations, a two-room, unheated summer cabin on Narragansett Bay. There we awaited contact from Alvin. It never came.

A week later I learned that his ship had sailed the night before we arrived—where, I didn't know. He was gone for many months, most of which he was unable to communicate with me. Yet all that time, I felt his influence in my life and was keenly aware of his love—and often it seemed to me that he was so close that I could almost hear his voice. That first week we were in Wickford, I had not known that he was already many hundreds of miles away. Had he died at sea, and for some reason the War Department had failed to notify me for several months, he would then have been dead the entire time I had thought of him as living. Would this fact have lessened my consciousness of his influence, curtailed my sense of his closeness, or made me less aware of his love?

The same sort of situation exists for many of us now. In this day and age so many of our friends and loved ones live with their families all over the globe. Does the fact that they may live hundreds or even thousands of miles away from us, so that many months go by without our seeing them, make them less needful of our prayers, or us of theirs? As being separated in life from our loved ones does not change or kill our relationship with them, neither does death.

This is not to say that physical separation is ever easy. It isn't, as we all know; it is never easy to walk entirely by faith and not by sight. But as in life we live in anticipation and expectation of our next reunion with those we love, so with death we live in the same "certain hope."

"He Has Been Touched"

During the initial period of my investigation of spiritual healing, many of the interviews I conducted were held at night after business hours, as the former patients, now recovered, were back at work. This meant leaving Alvin alone several times a week, and one evening, when I had an interview scheduled in a remote area, he volunteered to accompany me. He offered, as his avowed reason, that he did not want me to go so far alone at night, but I strongly suspected that his underlying motive was his growing curiosity.

Our destination was the home of a man reputedly healed of lung cancer. During some two hours Alvin sat unobtrusively in a corner of the room while I took notes of the man's story, procuring such data as the names of his doctors, what hospital he had been in, what laboratory tests had been conducted, and where and under what circumstances the alleged healing had taken place. Bright in my memory is the drive home—when after a long period of utter silence, I heard Alvin clear his throat and say: "You know, there may be something to this work you're doing, after all. Did you notice the radiance—the strange luminosity of that man's face? I don't know how to explain what I felt in him. All I'm sure of is that that man has been touched by something I don't know anything about."

He had been touched by Christ. Although we didn't know it then, Alvin was to receive the same touch and wear the same look—the sign of all who have known the presence of the Lord in this way.

In the beginning it had seemed fortuitous, and later on the mercy of God, that the healing ministry should have come within our ken at that precise time—for very shortly after, Alvin developed the extreme hypertension that eventually was to claim his life.

"Since he died," someone said to me, and probably a great many others have thought, "what good did the healing ministry do?"

The answer to this would fill many books. But, succinctly, the healing ministry did two things: First, and far, far above everything else in importance, it brought Alvin, as it brought me, to God. Second, there is no doubt whatsoever in my mind, as there was never any in his, that it was the power of God released through prayer that prolonged his life far beyond the normal expectancy of anyone in his physical situation. Three times within ten years doctors had told me, although not him, that he could not live more than a few months. Yet during all this time, with the exception of a mild heart ailment from which his recovery was complete, he never suffered a distressing symptom, was never in any way incapacitated, and very rarely missed a day at the office with so much as a cold. He was grateful for every day of his life, as am I.

During the last several years of his life, many people, both clergy and laity associated with the healing ministry, have stopped over in Pittsburgh to see us. Each time, Alvin received the laying-on of hands—always with spiritual benefit and frequently with physical.

One occasion which I shall long remember occurred following a dinner party we had given for an out-of-town guest. At our house that night were an Episcopal priest, a minister from the United Church of Christ, a Lutheran pastor, and a medical doctor. Just before they went home, prayer was offered for Alvin, and hands laid on together, in complete oneness of spirit and unity of faith in the healing Christ. The room was immediately filled this night with the result of God's presence: It was flooded with indescribable joy. This, then, was the joy of the Lord in all its fullness: The tremendous joy characteristic of the early Christians and too seldom manifested today. It is a joy that had its source not in the benefits received from God, but simply in the fact that God lives, and through Christ, we know it.

When the prayers were over, there was a long moment of deep silence, as we all rested in what was indeed a "holy hush." Then Alvin spoke quietly in a voice which seemed not his own: "Praise the Lord." To those who knew him as a reserved business executive, often embarrassed and always reticent concerning matters of the spirit, this was nearly as startling a manifestation of the Holy Spirit as the dramatic healing power of God. There flashed through my mind the words: "For he was a good man, and full of the Holy Ghost and of faith" (Acts 11:24).

As Alvin grew in faith and commitment, so did his concern increase, until it was scarcely less than mine, for those who turned to me for spiritual help. Often now, his first question on arriving home in the evening, was "Have you heard again from so-and-so?" And on more than one occasion, he was to say; "I've been thinking of that case you told me about last night. Let's pray together for them."

There came a time when Alvin's health seemed to me visibly to deteriorate, although his doctor professed no worry. Alvin began to look drawn and thin, and while I could never before remember his complaining of fatigue, he now admitted he was exhausted each evening when he came home. In addition he began to suffer increasingly frequent and severe attacks of angina.

In the early winter, at home with a bad cold, he had asked to see the completed portion of a book I then had in process on the healing ministry. It was my cardinal rule that no one, not even Alvin, ever read a word of script before it went to the publisher. Therefore I started to make a joking but nonetheless firm refusal, when I looked up into his eyes. I understood, then, that it was not boredom at being housebound with nothing to read, nor was it just idle curiosity that had prompted his request. I quickly handed him the completed chapters.

Within an hour he brought them back to me, with a smile. "Thanks, darling," he said. "This was just what I needed to strengthen my faith." This was the first inkling he had given me of his own discouragement.

He was obviously going downhill, and when sometimes his unguarded eyes met mine, I saw an expression there I had never seen before. Always in the habit of eagerly discussing future trips and plans, he showed the extent of his discouragement when he suddenly stopped speaking of or planning anything for the future. He had received the laying-on of hands. When I suggested that he be anointed, Alvin readily acquiesced.

Knowing that all the spiritual power we could garner was necessary at this time, we arranged for the sacrament on a Wednesday evening at eight o'clock when a number of local churches held their regular weekly healing services. He had long been on many prayer lists, but now I called the members of the various prayer groups, asking that each receive the laying-on of hands that night with special intention for Alvin. Many clergy of various church affiliations both in and out of Pittsburgh were called with the request that they be in prayer at that time. Thus, at the hour of anointing, prayer from many sources would be simultaneously offered. Those who are familiar with the healing ministry know from experience the tremendous spiritual power released in this way.

It seemed more than just coincidence that late on the night before the sacrament was to be administered, I received a telegram from a close friend, a surgeon, active in the healing ministry, stating that he was stopping over in Pittsburgh the following morning. When I told him of Alvin, and the anointing scheduled for that same evening, he saw in this unexpected visit, as I had, the hand of God.

From six o'clock that night when Alvin returned home from the office, until the priest arrived two hours later, we were all three in a more or less constant state of prayer, alternately praying alone and together; silently and vocally. By eight o'clock each one of us was keenly aware of the abundance of God's presence, and the atmosphere was electric with expectancy.

In order to save Alvin effort, the priest suggested that Alvin lie, or at least sit down, for the anointing, but he insisted upon kneeling. Thus flanked by the surgeon on one side and me on the other, he knelt to receive the healing sacrament. During the preliminary prayers, the power in the room seemed discernibly to mount until it climaxed at the moment of anointing. And at this moment the floor of the ordinary living room on which we knelt seemed to become "holy ground."

When Alvin arose from his knees, his face shone with that same indefinable but unmistakable radiance which he had first noted on another's face years before. "He has been touched by something I don't know anything about," he had said then. But now he knew.

Confrontation with Death

Alvin's conditioned worsened suddenly while he was in New York on a business trip. Emily flew from Pittsburgh to be with him in the hospital, where he remained for five days before returning home by train. Then, under strict medical supervision, he continued to go to his office for a few hours daily. Emily remained downtown during those hours, working on her current book at Trinity Cathedral.

This work routine of Alvin's continued for ten days, the most difficult days of our lives. Alvin was obviously very ill. He did not gain in strength, but persisted in going to the office, saying he felt better doing something than sitting around the house. He had always been courageous and outgoing, with a never-failing sense of humor, but now I was baffled by the complete change in him. While we had always been extremely close, during these days he withdrew from me completely, until there seemed no communication between us. I did not know it then, but already he was traversing a path I could not follow. This was the withdrawal of the dying, which I had seen before in others.

It was during these days that for the first time I actually understood with my heart something of the magnitude of God's love for the world—a love so great that he had sent his only Son to suffer for *us* that *we* might not perish. Suddenly I realized to an extent I never had before that our Lord's sacrifice neither began nor ended with the Crucifixion. Calvary could not be anchored to a specific date, but was the visible epitome for all time—past, present, and future—of Jesus' suffering. His death on Calvary was at once not only the consummation of the daily crucifixions preceding it, but the culmination of those that for nearly two thousand years have followed it, for with boundless love and limitless compassion, he *continues* to take our infirmities and bear our sicknesses.

The afternoon of the tenth day of his returning to work, Alvin called at the Cathedral, saying that he felt ill, and asking me to take him home immediately. That evening, in critical condition, he was taken by ambulance to the hospital.

Often when I have prayed for the healing of certain individuals, I have been conscious of a peculiar, positive assurance that they would recover. This night as I knelt to pray for Alvin, there swept over me more than a conviction—rather it was an irrevocable knowledge—that Alvin was going to die. I think I must have said "no" aloud, so incomprehensible was this to me just now—so vehement was my protest to God—so strong my rebellion.

How long I waged this battle I do not know, but suddenly I became intensely aware of God's presence. There was a momentary great stillness within me, and then I felt God's love wash over me. It seemed not so much an emotion as an almost palpable force cleansing, strengthening, driving before it all rebellion, all protest, all fear. Deeply impressed upon my understanding were the words, "Be not afraid." For a brief moment I knew nothing but the love of God and I caught a vision of the wholeness that lay in store for Alvin, a wholeness too complete for attainment on this earth.

The memory of this will remain with me always, and it eradicated all fear of death. Yet it was often difficult and sometimes impossible to recall with conviction the intensity of the experience as, in the days that followed, I watched Alvin die.

Through spiritual healing we seek the healing of the whole person—the total personality, body, mind, and spirit. But its primary goal is never the curing of the body but the healing of the spirit—bringing us into a closer relationship with God. This I knew Alvin had received, whatever the physical outcome. My every prayer opened and closed with praise and thanksgiving that this was so, for more clearly than ever before I recognized the wonder of such a healing. I never ceased to pray for Alvin's healing, according to God's will, in his own way and time and place, but the burden of my prayers was now that Alvin's soul might be more perfectly prepared; that his spirit and heart receive the full impact of God's healing power; that he know himself so wrapped in the love of Christ, and so filled with the Holy Spirit, that there would be no space within him to harbor fear or anxiety of any kind. This prayer was answered, for Alvin was neither anxious nor afraid, although I know that almost to the end, he wanted very much to live.

One night the doctor told me to summon our two married daughters from their respective homes in different states. At midnight I put in the calls.

Several considerations were involved, the first and abiding one, the danger of frightening the patient by summoning out-of-town members of the family. The girls and I discussed this aspect at length over the telephone, and we agreed on our "story": the girls had not seen each other since Christmas, and had decided to use Alvin's illness as an excuse, always eagerly sought, for a family get-together. Whether or not Alvin believed this, I never knew.

Diana's seven months' pregnancy had constituted an additional problem. Concerned over her, I had been loath to call her at all, but I knew she would never forgive me if I did not. I also knew the promise I had exacted of her, that she not come if her obstetrician advised against it, was worthless. Nothing on earth would have kept her from her father at this time.

Finally, I harbored a slight but real apprehension as to how our daughters would withstand the ordeal ahead of them. Much as I longed to have them with me for my sake as well as Alvin's, I was, in my fierce determination to protect him from any upset, almost afraid to have them come. To be sure, they had sounded calm and efficient over the telephone, but I knew their hearts were breaking. Both of them were unusually close to their father, and I only wondered if they could watch him die without going to pieces.

How little I knew my own children! I am ashamed now such doubt ever crept into my mind. After they came, I could only marvel at their emotional strength, their courage, their naturalness and cheerfulness with Alvin. They were magnificent in every way, and their selflessness, their submersion of their own grief in concern for me, their ceaseless effort to take care of me—to make me eat and rest—was a touching and wonderful thing. As I sat beside Alvin that last Friday afternoon, I marveled at his appearance of youth. It seemed strange that instead of being aged by this severe illness, he should look almost startlingly young.

The nurse came back from dinner, and noting Alvin's restlessness, prepared a hypodermic. I kissed him, and walked back to the solarium to join the girls— and as I walked there came into my mind, unbidden, the words of the Nunc Dimittis: "Lord, now lettest thou thy servant depart in peace, according to thy word: For mine eyes have seen thy salvation" (Luke 2:29-30).

We were getting ready to go home for an hour when I saw the nurse running down the corridor. I met her at the door. "He's gone," she said. I looked at her stupidly. "You mean he's *dead?*" and the word had a hollow, unreal sound. She nodded, the tears streaming down her face. She had loved him. We his family who loved him most stood there, dry-eyed, each momentarily isolated in her own grief too deep for tears.

I started down the hall to his room, the impulse strong to see him just once more, and then I realized the unwitting accuracy of the nurse's announcement. "He's gone," she had said, and of course he was. Suddenly I felt him close—closer than he had been in weeks, and with a closeness stronger than any physical bond. I remember my soaring joy, and the thought, "If this is death, I wonder why people dread it so."

On the morning of the funeral as we walked out to the car waiting to take us to the church, I suddenly felt God near. I remember how on the last Sunday he was home, Alvin had wanted to go to church, but since he was obviously not well, I had dissuaded him and gone on alone. I had not known that the last time we would go to church together on this earth would be in this way.

"I am the resurrection and the life, saith the Lord: he that believeth in me, though he were dead, yet shall he live: and whosoever liveth and believeth in me, shall never die" (John 11:25-26).

"I know that my Redeemer liveth ... and though this body be destroyed, yet shall I see God ... and not as a stranger" (Job 19:25-27). Hearing these words as I entered the church, my heart suddenly surged with a great gladness. Then I had to focus on only one thing: the mundane task of getting to the front of the church. It seemed the longest walk I had ever taken.

More than anything else I had wanted a requiem mass, but lurking in the back of my mind was the fear that receiving Holy Communion, however much I wanted to, might prove an unendurable emotional ordeal. Yet I, who had claimed to know something of

God's love and mercy, should have known better, for this was to prove so wonderful an experience that it would color and influence my life from that day forward.

In the ensuing brief moments, it seems to me I lived a lifetime of personal religious experience that was to transform a phrase in the creed—a formerly little-understood theological doctrine—into a living and fully realizable actuality. *I believe in the communion of saints.* At that moment, words that I had often repeated with little thought now sprang into life. This, then, was what they meant.

As our Lord was truly present in the sacrament, so was Alvin truly near me now, separated only by the thinnest of veils woven of my own physical senses. With complete conviction I knew we worshiped now, together, in the presence of God, as we always had. Simultaneously I seemed to comprehend that, as throughout our marriage we had helped one another, so could we continue now through our mutual prayers, and as throughout our marriage we had loved one another, so did our love go on, undestroyed by death.

This was the day above all others in my life that I was to thank God most fervently for the gift of faith. This was the day when I learned with more than my mind that the Eucharist is the Christ-appointed meeting place of the faithful throughout the ages, both living and dead, yet all alive. It is the place where we know ourselves surrounded by God's saints, by, as the book of Hebrews says, that cloud of unseen witnesses, who continually guide and love and help.

This was the day on which (because it was first so powerfully experienced) there was forever engraved in my heart the full and wonderful portent of the words from the prayer book: "Therefore with angels and arch-angels, and with all the company of heaven, we laud and magnify thy glorious Name. . . ."

The church that day was filled with those who had loved Alvin, and many were to tell me later what the service had meant to them. "If only we had done this when Jim died instead of the service at the funeral home," said one woman, "I think my entire reaction to his death would have been different." Another, unfamiliar with the Episcopal Church, whose child had died two years before, was to say: "This was the first time I have felt any real comfort since losing Tommy." I remember also being startled later by the comment of an elderly gentleman who remarked: "I've been to a lot of funerals, but *never to one in a church*. It makes such a difference." I don't know why his remark should have surprised me. I, too, had never before in my life been to a church funeral.

I can remember years ago wondering how the bereaved could survive a church funeral, with their grief openly exposed to the gaze of many strangers. It seemed to me then that the funeral home custom of a private room for the family, with the service being piped in over a loudspeaker, was a far more humane arrangement. Furthermore, it certainly seemed less hard on the family to go directly from there to the cemetery, rather than drawing out the agony by an intermediate stop at a church.

Possibly this completely mistaken idea of mine is still harbored by many churchgoers, even faithful ones. But if only they could know the strength and solace their church could bring, I think few would choose any place *except* a church for this last service.

Every religiously significant event in the lives of Christians takes place in a church. It is there we are baptized and confirmed; it is there we receive Holy Communion, and most of us are married. It seems curious that the last and most important earthly event should so frequently be observed apart from the church, thereby withholding its final complete blessing from the spirit of the deceased, and its strengthening consolation from the bereaved.

Doctrines of Death and Life

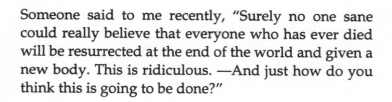

After the funeral Emily found her daughters full of questions, the most poignant of which was "Where is Daddy now?" In dealing with this question, which expresses a universal concern about our departed loved ones, she answered her daughters with the teaching of the church regarding judgment and "the final resurrection, in which we shall be raised and given new spiritual bodies."

Emily did not then, nor did she ever, pretend to have all the answers to the mysteries of death and eternal life. But she believed the teachings of Jesus and trusted in the example of his Resurrection.

Someone said to me recently, "Surely no one sane could really believe that everyone who has ever died will be resurrected at the end of the world and given a new body. This is ridiculous. —And just how do you think this is going to be done?"

I haven't the remotest idea. But I believe it, and it seems no more remarkable than the other miracles on which the faith is founded: the Incarnation, the Resurrection, the Ascension, and the sending of the Holy Ghost. The entire Christian faith is a miracle—above all Jesus' ministry and his life, which continues in us today. If I disbelieved all I do not understand of Christianity, I would not claim it; and unless I believed it all, whether or not I understand it, I could not claim it.

As a Christian I must believe in the general resurrection because it fulfills the doctrine taught and exemplified by our Lord: A doctrine unique among religions.

"Behold my hands and my feet, that it is I myself," Jesus said (Luke 24:39), when after his resurrection he appeared to the frightened apostles who thought they had seen a ghost. "Handle me, and see; for a spirit hath not flesh and bones, as ye see me have." This, in essence, is the Christian doctrine of resurrection. It is not the absorption of the soul into the divine, as taught by some great religions; not the deathlessness of a disembodied spirit floating ghost-like through all eternity; but the raising to eternal life of the *complete* personality, consisting of body as well as soul.

During the forty days between the Resurrection and the Ascension, our Lord made many appearances. He did not come as a vision, present with his disciples only in spiritual power, nor yet in the form of a resuscitated physical body, but as Saint Paul tries to explain it, in a "natural body . . . raised a spiritual body" (1 Cor. 15:44). Although incorruptible and above the limitations of the earthly body, Christ's resurrected body is still identifiable to those who love him.

The empty tomb pointed to the Resurrection. The appearance of Jesus afterwards demonstrated for all time the completeness of his victory over death—not only for himself, but for all of us.

"I'm a Christian but I don't believe in life after death," I heard a man remark recently. Actually, this is an impossible contradiction. The precise *nature* of survival may be open to conjecture, for "it doth not yet appear what we shall be" (1 John 3:2); but the question of *whether* the dead survive is not open to the Christian. Otherwise the entire gospel is invalidated, for the resurrection of our Lord is denied: "If there be no resurrection of the dead, then is Christ not risen: And if Christ be not risen, then is our preaching vain, and your faith is also vain" (1 Cor. 15:13-14).

Concerning the state of our dead, our prayer that "the souls of the departed may rest in peace" bothers many of us. It used to bother me until I came to believe that their "rest shall be glorious" (Isa. 11:10). As one woman put it, whose son, a dynamic and vital young man, had died following surgery: "I just can't bear to think of him as merely *resting*. He was too full of life—too energetic."

But we do not believe that our dead are in a state of passive inactivity. As one of the saints has said: "No one rests until he toils for Thee." We pray that our dead rest in God. That is not stagnation, but the "peace which passeth all understanding," which here we have only glimpsed; not sterility, but a perfect and growing life in Christ, free from all busyness, but busy; free from all senseless activity, but active in a reaching towards God, unimpeded and unfrustrated by sin. Surely there is no barrenness for those who are able to receive without human limitation the beneficence and benevolence of God.

A few weeks ago, a grief-stricken woman spoke to me of the death of her husband. She expressed what seems to me among the most common—and what would seem the most terrible—of all grief reactions: the *fear* of the living for their dead.

"I can't sleep," she said, "because I worry so that he is not all right: that he may be suffering, or unhappy and lonely."

I can't conceive of a greater agony than to live in a state of perpetual apprehension as to the fate of one we love. Surely one of the most wonderful consequences of holding a deep faith before death occurs is to circumvent a corroding fear of this kind.

"How can I know he's safe?" she went on, in frustrated bitterness. "We have absolutely nothing to go on: nothing to sustain or reassure us."

Nothing?

"Eye hath not seen, nor ear heard, neither have entered into the heart of man, the things which God hath prepared for them that love him" (1 Cor. 2:9).

"They shall hunger no more, neither thirst any more; neither shall the sun light on them, nor any heat. For the Lamb which is in the midst of the throne shall feed them, and shall lead them unto living fountains of waters: and God shall wipe away all tears from their eyes" (Rev. 7:16-17).

But most of all and above all else, Jesus' pledge, "That where I am, there ye may be also" (John 14:3), and his promise, "Today shalt thou be with me in paradise" (Luke 23:43). When all is said and done, this is all we really know of life after death—and it is enough.

There are those who say that death is the end. But for the Christian, the end of human life is not death, but the resurrection, and never was I more thrillingly sure of this than on the following Easter, less than four weeks after Alvin's death. The words, *For he is risen, as he said* (Matt. 28:6), echoed over and over again in my brain, until quite suddenly my mind seemed to apprehend their implication, my heart to grasp their meaning, and my spirit to know their truth. At this instant I experienced something of the joy and excitement of the apostles when they learned the tomb was empty.

It is curious that, although the entire Christian faith rests upon the actuality of the Resurrection, no aspect of the faith seems so little believed in our hearts. We seem to be forever stuck between the Nativity and the Crucifixion. Yet if the evidence of his resurrection is carefully studied, it seems to me more difficult to disbelieve than to believe. Consider also the fact that twelve disillusioned and grief-stricken men, faced with what they thought was the failure of their Lord, were so convinced of the truth of his resurrection that they spent the rest of their lives undergoing torture, persecution, and martyrdom in order to proclaim it. The church was born not because Jesus lived and taught, but because he died and rose.

Means of Grace

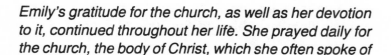

Emily's gratitude for the church, as well as her devotion to it, continued throughout her life. She prayed daily for the church, the body of Christ, which she often spoke of

as "the extension of the Incarnation." In the following pages Emily reveals what it meant to her at the time of her bereavement and after.

In response to the news of Alvin's death, a clergyman wrote to me and said, "In all your speaking and writing you so continually emphasize the church. I am curious to know what it has meant to you in this time of trouble."

Words are wholly inadequate to describe what the church has meant and continues to mean. I only attempt the impossible, so that someone else to whom it may mean less will seek and find what has been so abundantly given me and is offered to all who kneel at her altar rail: the all-enfolding love of God, the joy of the real presence of our Lord, the inestimable comfort of the Holy Spirit—all intensified, all magnified, all vividly experienced.

When I decided to move after Alvin's death, my primary, indeed my sole, consideration had been proximity to the church. I felt instinctively that no matter what happened, if the church were easily accessible, I could cope with and bear anything. In the months that have passed, the rightness of this decision has been confirmed far beyond even my greatest expectations.

After a bereavement many people find it difficult or even impossible to attend church for a long time afterwards—not because they don't want to go, but because the emotional impact of the service is too great. I know myself singularly blessed that this was not the case with me, for from the first moment the church has been my greatest solace. The only thing I could not have borne would have been to be deprived of what she offers so abundantly.

Clearly, without an intensely personal relationship with God, the church and her liturgy must be a travesty. Conversely, however (or so it seems to me) a purely personal relationship with God *without* the church would be at best a stunted, partial thing, always incapable of fulfillment without the means of grace offered in prayers, the Word, and the sacraments.

"But prayer is not confined to the church," you say. "We pray at home, too." Yes, but for the Christian all prayer must be church-centered. The Christian never prays alone, but always as a member of Christ's Body within the communion of saints.

"But the Word is not limited to the church," you object. "We read it for ourselves at all times and in all places." Yes, but the church is its custodian and agent.

We can experience God through prayer, and we can learn about God through the Word—but we receive God in the sacrament of Holy Communion, ordained for this specific purpose. There are some who, in their emphasis on the Word alone, infer that this great sacrament is largely an invention of the church, but the fact is that many years before the Gospels were recorded, the breaking of the bread was done in accordance with Christ's command.

The reality of Christ's presence at the Eucharist is a very different thing from the sense of the nearness and presence of God we feel when we pray and meditate. Our experience of Christ, wholly present in the sacrament of the altar, cannot be explained, but neither can it be explained away.

The Holy Spirit indeed "maketh intercession . . . according to the will of God" (Rom. 8:27). Kneeling before the Blessed Sacrament, the act of adoration becomes involuntarily an act of reconsecration and rededication, and as in the offering of myself Christ gives himself to me, the anguish never fails to recede. I can feel it literally ebb out of me, to be replaced by a sensation of inexpressible joy. Suddenly all that matters is my love for God, even more than God's love for me. Worshiping is not a means to an end but an end in itself—a "naked intention" directed towards God: Seeking only the giver and not the gift . . . and somehow receiving both.

As God is not dependent on me, but I am on God, so the church does not need me, but I need her. As a crutch? No. But as the source of the Holy Spirit, as the guardian and interpreter of the faith, as the extension of the Incarnation, I need her means of grace, her prayers, her spiritual power.

This is not to imply that the operation of the Holy Spirit is confined to the church, but that the church is the fountainhead; it is not to imply that the church can create faith in a human heart, but that she can impart the faith, to which, by God's action on each soul, we are enabled to respond. Solitary Christian experience is not invalid, but the church is the instrument appointed by God through which God's manifold wisdom is revealed. And the church is also the instrument through which God's power is most abundantly received. As I have seen this strikingly demonstrated in the healing ministry, so has it been manifested in my own life.

I must admit that I am now so oriented to the church that in a sense I do not exist without her, but this was not always so. At one time, and not too long ago, I leaned strongly towards the intense individualism that tends to eschew the church as the bearer of revelation and salvation in favor of purely personal experience. Not until I gradually realized that the most profound religious experience had come to me always within the context of the church, did I begin to recognize her as a reservoir of incalculable spiritual power. It was then that I retreated from the isolation of my individualism and became a dependent member of the Body of which Christ is the head.

I could hear my own voice of a few years ago, in the recent comment of a woman angry with her minister over a supposed slight: "At a time when I needed it most," she said indignantly, "the church has let me down." Her pastor perhaps, but not the church; the church will *never* let us down. Regardless of the imperfections of any given church, and I am well aware of these, the church remains the agency Christ has commissioned to preach and to teach and to heal in his name, by the power of the Holy Ghost. Jesus made it very clear that faith is not a private affair.

The church has offered me solace. I have gone to her depleted and been replenished. I have gone to her desolate and found comfort. I have gone to her spiritually hungry and received the Bread of Life. Through her means of grace I have known the limitless power of the Holy Spirit, the boundless love of Christ, and the infinite glory of God. No one could ask for more.

Facing the Future

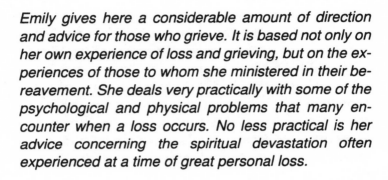

Emily gives here a considerable amount of direction and advice for those who grieve. It is based not only on her own experience of loss and grieving, but on the experiences of those to whom she ministered in their bereavement. She deals very practically with some of the psychological and physical problems that many encounter when a loss occurs. No less practical is her advice concerning the spiritual devastation often experienced at a time of great personal loss.

For a long time I had a professional life of my own as well as my life with Alvin. Therefore I must admit to being totally unprepared upon his death for my devastating sense of inadequacy and incompleteness, for the apparent loss of my own identity, for the sensation of somehow being severed from myself—the feeling that I, too, had died.

Actually none of these reactions should have been surprising. A long and happily married couple have, in a very real sense, become one. Separation by death does violence to this oneness, rending the personality of the survivor in half. That person does not merely *feel* less than whole, but in many respects *is* less than whole. And the first step in readjustment must be to regain that lost identity: To learn who the "I" that once was, and is no longer, has now become.

When any human being whom we have known dies,

each of us who lives dies a little also—to what extent is determined by the closeness of that relationship.

I have perceived in my own "dying" a reason for the pervading presence of God with which I have been so continually blessed from the beginning: As Alvin by his physical death has come into God's nearer presence, so have I by my smaller death come closer to God than ever before, experiencing his reality and life to a degree that I had never thought possible on this earth.

Recognizing the problems

Regardless of our faith, we are all human, and every one of us can expect to be confronted with certain problems arising from our involuntary psychological reactions to death. The first problem which beset me, and indeed the one from which many others derived, was that of oversensitivity. For a short time I was absurdly hurt by what people said and did, and equally hurt by what they failed to do and say. I wanted love and dreaded pity, yet when I was offered the first I too often mistook it for the second. I refused to accept invitations to do things with people lest I had been asked only because people were sorry for me. And when those whom I had liked but scarcely knew quite understandably failed to concern themselves with me, I felt hurt and slighted.

This kind of unhappiness generated by inconsequentials seems to be a common phenomenon of readjustment. The fact that I knew my reactions to be foolish and irrational did not help. All that *did* help was prayer. As I placed my entire confidence in God, the abnormal sensitivity receded, until human relationships became normal again.

Part of that hypersensitivity was the almost obsessive determination not to be a nuisance to friends—not to be dependent upon, or in any way indebted to them. A close friend finally set me straight. This kind and spirit-filled doctor had offered me something that under ordinary circumstances I would have accepted with pleasure and thanks and thought no more about. Now I refused it in no uncertain terms. He looked at me hard for a moment, and then he said: "This is all your pride, Emily. It's true that our Lord said, 'It is more blessed to give than to receive,' but it is also necessary to know how to receive. You don't—and this is something you've got to learn."

I saw the truth of his statement and suddenly realized my unwillingness to accept was due to false pride, and that all such hypersensitivity is due largely to self-centeredness.

The culprits once identified, the way was clear. Laying my pride and egotism at God's feet, my prayer became, "Forgive me these sins," and as God answered with absolving grace, my attitude dramatically changed. But another battle remained to be fought before the war was won.

For a brief time I found myself engaged in a struggle against bitter resentment, when it seemed to me that many of my friends were joined in a deliberate conspiracy of silence where Alvin was concerned, apparently thinking, or so I believed, that if they could forget that he had ever lived, they could then forget that he had died.

I loved to speak of him, for it kept him close, and tried to do so frequently, always casually and unemotionally. And then I began to see pain flicker across the faces of friends. I noted the too-quick plunge into another subject; the way his name seemed to hang in the air, suspended in an atmosphere of discomfiture, until with all except our closest friends, I ceased to mention him at all.

The reluctance of friends and even relatives to mention the dead is due, first, perhaps, to embarrassment and apprehension lest a flood of tears be released; and, second, to a general misconception among those who have never lost by death anyone extremely close, that to speak of the deceased will cause pain. Nothing could be further from the truth. To the one who has loved the most, it is the greatest possible comfort.

The first day with Diana, I mentioned Alvin as casually as I might have had he been at home while I visited the children. Her face brightened with relief, and she exclaimed, "Oh, I'm *so* glad you're able to talk of Daddy like this. Bill [her young husband] and I sat up half the night trying to decide whether talking of him would hurt you. We so want to keep his memory alive to the children."

I understood then and with considerable shame that what I had resented in some of my friends as a selfish conspiracy of silence on their parts was, in fact, due only to their fear I would be hurt. Thus my resentment became gratitude that they had sought, however mistakenly, to protect me.

Whether the bereaved is a man or woman, surely one of the most difficult emotional adjustments to make is to the fact that now you are no longer "first" with anyone. When we are confronted with this realization, we tend to lose our motivation, and while some may plunge headlong into more and harder work in order to mitigate their pain, others can scarcely force themselves to work at all.

Men and women alike suffer this temporary loss of motivation caused by loss of the companion who cares most deeply. I think it is only in your spirit's cognizance of your true status as a child of God that your sense of belonging will be restored and your seemingly lost purpose regained. For the believer, the way to this cognizance, as to everything else, lies in prayer.

Emily speaks also of the remorse that follows any death. The survivor feels intensely sorry for many things: words hastily spoken, words not spoken, lost opportunities to express love. In her case, the one deep regret was that she did not acknowledge to her husband that she knew he was dying, "So that we might have shared together his last and greatest experience as we had shared everything else in our lives until that point."

I remember so well how, six months before Alvin went to the hospital, I casually advised a woman to speak to her husband of his impending death. How little I understood then the magnitude of the task that I had so glibly assigned her. I know now better than ever before how good my advice to her had been—but when it came to myself, I couldn't take it.

It wasn't that I didn't give the matter thought (there was hardly an hour of any day while he was in the hospital that I didn't ponder it). But how do you say it? Do you look at your husband, whom you want so desperately to save all worry and apprehension, and say, "Darling, perhaps you don't know it, but you're dying"? I *couldn't*, because I was never sure he knew until that day I saw the unalloyed longing in his eyes as he looked out the window. That night I made my decision: The next day I would by some sign, even if not by word, let him know that I knew.

The next morning his nurse met me outside the door: "Mr. Neal has just made me promise," she said, "that I will not let you know the progress of his illness."

These words ended forever any possibility of my telling him. His final gift to me was an effort to save me worry—and I accepted it. I could only wish now, when it is too late, that I had given him in return a greater gift—my refusal to accept his.

In a culture that fears death and reacts with anxiety and distaste to its very mention, that seeks to obscure its reality, that rejects the word *death*, substituting such euphemisms as "passing away" or "departed," in such a culture the Christian could make a telling witness of the faith. And yet how often we fail, and so did I. I shall be sorry always that I did not speak. But Alvin knows why I failed to say those things—and how much I wish I had.

Spiritual disciplines

I am grateful that before my husband died, the habit of thanksgiving had become firmly entrenched in me, leading to a sustained consciousness of God's presence. During the past months I have seen the spiritual law involved in gratitude remarkably fulfilled. Instinctively beginning the day with a prayer of thanksgiving for a good night's sleep—or if I haven't slept, for the undisturbed hours in which to think—the habitual sense of gratitude increases as the day goes on, climaxing always in the supreme thankfulness that God lives, and that I know it. Because of this, I am somehow grateful even for my own suffering, for through it I know myself closer to Christ.

Since Alvin's death I have learned, to a degree I never appreciated before, the importance of spiritual discipline; for emotion, at best, is erratic, and after the shock of death, totally untrustworthy.

As the months have passed, I have talked with many despairing men and women whose suffering has been tragically intensified by what they have discovered to be their paucity of faith when put to the test. The imperative need is not only for a fervent but for a *well-grounded* faith, built not on the quicksand of pure emotion but stabilized by spiritual discipline. Christianity should not be regarded as a "crisis" religion. An intelligent and steadfast faith usually cannot be acquired overnight, nor can most of us instantaneously glean a knowledge of God. If we turn to Christ only when we are in despair, it is not that he will ever fail to offer us consolation, but that we, totally unprepared, are too often unable to receive him.

There are few of us, whatever our circumstances or our activities or our family responsibilities, who could not spend more time than we do on matters of the spirit. Most of us, leading harassed and busy lives, point to lack of time as an excuse. The vast majority of the bereaved, however, are those whose children are grown and away from home, and their problem now is not too little time but too much time on their hands. I can't think of a more fruitful way to spend it than in exploring the field of the spirit. In attempting to live a more spiritually disciplined life than you have lived before, in your effort to be more obedient to Christ and to his church, you will come closer to God than you have ever been, and your burden of grief will be eased beyond your greatest expectation.

The Christian faith as I understand it is not mere acquiescence, or the performance of good works; it is a passion for Christ and a compelling need to serve him. It is not a mundane Sunday morning routine, but a joyous seven-days-a-week experience. It is not a sedative, although it brings peace, but a stimulant that keeps us in a state of "divine discontent." Above all, the faith is not a narcotic. It does not offer us freedom from pain, but the promise that Christ is always with us.

If you are bereaved and your faith is unshaken, witness to God's glory. If your faith is temporarily shaken and weak, consider joining a prayer group, where you will find people who are living a vital faith and daily demonstrating its fruits. Their faith will bolster yours, and their love, the love of God in action, will sustain and comfort you.

And if you have no faith, but for the first time seek God—if, as G. K. Chesterton expresses it, you are experiencing "the first wild doubt of doubt"—try accepting the hypothesis that there *is* a God. Remind yourself that although you cannot see love, you know that it *exists;* that although you cannot see suffering, you know that it *is;* that although you have never seen neurons and protons, you know that they are. Seek God, and you will know the promise fulfilled that will change your life. "And ye shall seek me, and find me, when ye shall search for me with all your heart" (Jer. 29:13).

Study the gospels with whatever prayer you are capable of offering, that you may understand with your heart the words your eyes read. Where should you begin? Perhaps with Saint John, whose account seems to me so wonderfully filled with the love, and illumined by the light, of Christ.

Regardless of the quality of your faith, surround yourself as much as you can with believers. As you realize you are now more dependent on God than you have ever been before, you will turn to the church with perhaps a new humility and a clearer vision of her as Christ's mystical Body containing his truth and his power and his life.

Assent to the teaching of the church, and you will see for possibly the first time the full extent of its bearing on your personal problems. Open wide your heart to God who forgives through the church, to Christ who speaks through her, and to the Holy Spirit who enables through her. And if for a while you find it difficult to pray, let "Lord have mercy upon me" be your only prayer. It is enough, and you will find it marvelously answered. All that is necessary is that you fix your heart on Christ, and you will receive more than his consolation—you will know the miracle of his joy.

The Ministry of Death

Emily has expressed her deep gratitude for the church's teachings and sacraments, which sustained

her so wonderfully after Alvin's death. Here she suggests some ways in which both clergy and lay church members could strengthen their ministry to the bereaved.

The ministry of death is as generally neglected by the church as the ministry of healing and with equally disastrous results. Embedded in every human heart are certain longings. The answer to all of these, as to every other such need with which we are confronted, lies in Jesus; and the church, through him, holds these answers if only she will teach them. When she does not, people desperate for comfort will turn elsewhere, without knowing that the church offers them the communion of saints.

Regardless of faith, it is a universal yearning of the bereaved to be assured that death is not the total end of the relationship they once knew, and that some sort of communion with their beloved dead is possible. On the authority of Scripture, and by faith, the church supplies us the means through Christ by which this spiritual union can be attained.

Recently I was present at a meeting of an interdenominational prayer group, all of whom were devout church members and most of whom stood each Sunday to recite the creed. Yet when someone broached the subject of the communion of saints, not one person in the group had the remotest idea what it means. Where, then, is the church, that she so seldom instructs on this article of the faith? Why does she so universally neglect every aspect of the ministry of death?

If mediums and spiritualists refuse to let their dead die, the church refuses to let our dead live, by apparently joining forces with society in its attempt to shield us from the reality of death—seeming to believe that if we overlook it, it will go away.

Discussions are constantly underway as to how the church may be made more relevant to the needs of our present culture. As a member of this culture, I submit that the "faith once for all delivered to the saints" meets (as it has from the beginning, and will until the end) our every need. But it must be taught—whole, undiluted, and unweakened by compromise.

Certainly among the most important of doctrines are those concerned with death and beyond: The Resurrection and the Ascension, the communion of saints, the fact that Jesus victoriously overcame death for all eternity and for each one of us now. This is the good news—the very foundation of the faith—and yet it is so inadequately taught and so little understood and believed, that the atheist and the average Christian are totally indistinguishable in their fearful reaction to death.

I suspect that sermons on death are not very popular with some parishioners, who would prefer not to think about the subject. But the church is not engaged in a popularity contest, and when she neglects her responsibility in the ministry of death, she weakens the Christian faith.

In the specific area of death, Christ's love, help, and comfort are tangibly expressed in our ministry to the bereaved. It would seem to me entirely possible that a knowledgeable and compassionate ministration in this field might well spell the difference between very real sickness and health, between dangerously abnormal grief reactions and normal ones. I know the value of this ministry, for I am bereaved; I know its difficulties, for since Alvin died many have come to me in search of help; and I know the lack of preparation of the average clergy in this important field, for I have heard so many of their anxious questions.

One young minister at a religious conference expressed a typical uncertainty when he said, "Right now there is someone in my parish I'd like to help; her husband died a couple of weeks ago, but what should I do? She seems surrounded by family and friends, and I don't want to intrude." I think my answer would be common to many who are in the first stage of active grief: "A minister never intrudes. When you visit the bereaved, as when you visit the sick, you take to them the greatest of gifts: the power of God called forth by prayer."

When the pastor of his first church said to me in all sincerity, "I'd *run* all the way across town to minister to someone who needs me, but isn't it better to wait until I'm called?" I could only answer: "If you *know* someone is in need, you've already *been* called. Don't make them telephone you—just go."

I know how sensitive the bereaved can be, and how often absurdly proud, how inadequate they feel, and how desperate their need of reassurance, concern, love. Give it to them as "ministers of God, in much patience, in afflictions, in necessities, in distresses . . ." (2 Cor. 6:4). Don't force them to ask you for it.

The clergy are human, and some are unable to handle a grief situation as well as others, most often perhaps because of some inner barrier to compassion. They may lack love, and if so, they cannot give what they do not have. One of the great difficulties of this ministry is that empathy is far more valuable to the bereaved than mere sympathy. As one man who has been in the ministry for years admitted, "I never knew the meaning of grief or how to treat it until I suffered a death in my own family a short while ago."

For those who are clergy, it has been suggested that they make frequent calls for a period of about a month and then gradually withdraw. Regardless of what the clergy may think, house calls are never a waste of time for the bereaved, and they can be made creative through prayer. Prayer, of course, is the answer. It means much to us that our pastor has cared enough to call, but we all need prayer at all times—and particularly during a period of distress when it is often impossible for us to pray for ourselves. If we do not ask for prayer, it does not mean that we do not badly want it. So, please, offer it for us, unasked. However great our faith may appear, we all need the church's ministry.

Six months ago a man in a small Midwestern town suffered a heart attack. He was rushed to the hospital, and his priest, who was on the golf links with three of the church's vestrymen, was summoned. Within half an hour he was at the bedside of the sick man, and his three golfing companions, who had immediately left the links, were at the hospital, standing by to give their services if needed. As they waited, they called their wives and asked them to arrange to babysit—all night if necessary—the sick man's children.

The man died early the next morning, and the whole church turned up to help the widow, who had recently been under psychiatric care. Not for a day or two, but for weeks, church members visited her in shifts, so that unless she wished, she needed never be alone. She received help with her children and constant spiritual help from her priest, whose ministry had planted in her the faith she needed to withstand this blow.

This is the church's ministry of death in action: the mystical body and its members, through which the love of Christ is manifested. I have termed this ministry of the church *the ministry of death,* but more accurately it is *the ministry of life.* In its fullest sense, it is a healing ministry—requiring the same daring and the same dynamic faith, the same love and the same compassion, which by the power of the Holy Spirit and in the name of Jesus, makes whole all brokenness.

CHAPTER FIVE

Encounters on the Road
Spreading the Healing Word

———————◆———————

Emily's fifth book, Where There's Smoke, *is based on her experiences as a healing missioner during the mid-1960s. In this mission work she traveled throughout the country to speak at churches of many denominations. As part of each mission, Emily conducted open sessions in which she took questions from the floor. Through the years, these interactions with the large crowds who attended her missions led her deeply into the basic issues arising in the ministry of healing. This chapter describes some of them:*

- *her dealings with the inevitable skepticism of nonbelievers*

- *her pursuit of Christian unity in overcoming denominational barriers*

- *her perception of Holy Communion as the church's chief service of healing and wholeness*

- *her cooperative engagement with physicians and others of the medical community*

During the period of mission work described here, Emily Gardiner Neal was in her fifties. She continued active in this work until well into her seventies, by which time she had reduced her schedule to one mission each month. Nonetheless, each mission still involved the rigors of travel and long hours of public speaking and ministry. These efforts depleted her physical strength but energized her inwardly. She felt called to missioning and gave it up reluctantly just two years before her death.

Here Emily describes briefly the structure of her mission work.

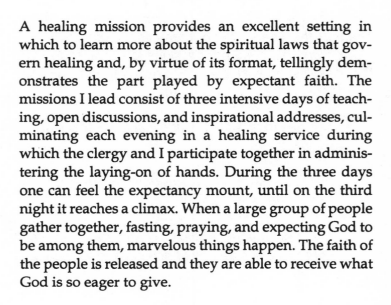

A healing mission provides an excellent setting in which to learn more about the spiritual laws that govern healing and, by virtue of its format, tellingly demonstrates the part played by expectant faith. The missions I lead consist of three intensive days of teaching, open discussions, and inspirational addresses, culminating each evening in a healing service during which the clergy and I participate together in administering the laying-on of hands. During the three days one can feel the expectancy mount, until on the third night it reaches a climax. When a large group of people gather together, fasting, praying, and expecting God to be among them, marvelous things happen. The faith of the people is released and they are able to receive what God is so eager to give.

After traveling all over the nation, talking to and with people of every educational level and in every stage of belief and disbelief, I have observed a great hunger. The hunger is not for intellectual answers to religious questions, that the mind may be satisfied, but for a personal experience of the living God, that the soul may be fulfilled.

Responding to Skeptics

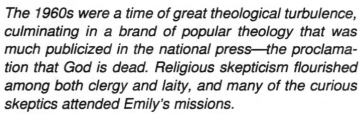

The 1960s were a time of great theological turbulence, culminating in a brand of popular theology that was much publicized in the national press—the proclamation that God is dead. Religious skepticism flourished among both clergy and laity, and many of the curious skeptics attended Emily's missions.

Her responses to skeptical queries often took the form of stating, simply and in current terms, some of the principal doctrines of the Christian faith. The reason for this is that she viewed the healing ministry as an integral part of Christianity, grounded firmly in scriptural accounts of Christ's teachings, his healing acts, and his commissioning of those who followed him. The ministry of healing was further validated by widespread practice in the early church, as she has described earlier. Therefore, she never saw this ministry as an interesting but optional church program. She saw it as embedded in the total Christian story.

Speaking from her position of undaunted orthodoxy, Emily returned again and again to the doctrinal basics that undergird the church's healing ministry. She be-

gins here by addressing the crisis of meaninglessness and the prevailing worship of intellect. She brings into play all parts of the Anglican "three-legged stool": scripture, tradition, and reason—as well as the powerful testimony of her continuing experience with physical cures, spiritual healings, and changed lives.

The universal disease (it is far from new, only more acute today) is meaninglessness. In the interest of total health, we need to discern meaning in our lives. We have in the United States more material prosperity than ever before, yet we have the highest rate in history of divorce, juvenile delinquency, mental illness, and general discontent. The same sickness—meaninglessness—afflicts both sexes, and the remedy is the same for both: Jesus Christ.

Psychologists speak of the numbers of psychically displaced persons who are unable to relate to others or themselves. They are lost personalities, unable to find themselves, to achieve identity. In contrast, those men and women who have given their lives without reservation to Christ are singularly free from this prevalent crisis of identity. They know that Christ must come first in every Christian home and that, when he does, the love between members of that family grows deeper than it ever was before. As their relationships with each other grow more profound, so do their concern and sensitivity toward others; in the love of Jesus we conceive an infinite love for all souls. They recognize that Christians are called upon to be intercessors, not only by prayer, but in some cases, by being present with someone who is suffering. They are never "too busy."

Such practicing Christians are people of courage, for they are not ashamed to profess the Lord Jesus to a hostile world or to witness to the gospel in an unbelieving one. Their lives have meaning, and they know well what it is.

These people are not a few esoteric souls with nothing better to do than pray, but vigorous and dynamic representatives of the whole of society. They represent every age, cultural background, level of education, color, but they all are bound together by the strongest of all bonds: The spiritual one, Christ.

These people are far from perfect, like everyone else. But they have all learned something of the meaning of love and something of God from whom all love is derived. In the knowledge that they belong not to themselves, but to God, they have found true fulfillment and the joy that no person can give and none can take from them. Above all, they have learned to put first things first. They do not worship worldly success, but worship God. Their primary desire is not to become corporation presidents (although some are), but to be God's servants. They see in serving God the purpose of their lives.

In this era of intellect-worship, no one knows better than I the prodigious difficulty of simple faith, of overcoming our propensity to substitute *thinking* about God for *experiencing* God. We rationalize, we equivocate, we torture the Gospel, because anything and everything is easier than simple faith. But eventually we come to know the truth: Things of the spirit cannot be apprehended solely by the mind, no matter how great the intellect (1 Cor. 2:14).

The religious iconoclast and the traditional Christian do share a common goal: the discovery of truth. The difference lies in the method of search and the conclusion to which each comes. Among the iconoclast's most basic problems seems to be the question of where God is. The conclusion that he is not "up there" or out in space scarcely comes as a surprise to the instructed Christian. However, the insistence of the "modern" theologian that God is solely in our hearts results in the rejection of the exalted Lord, presumably all forms of prayer, and, in fact, the Christian faith. Unless we concede God's otherness as well as his indwelling, we simply are not Christians.

Today's revamping of the faith overlooks a basic psychological need: the need to worship. As the re-imaging of God is presumably to lead the unchurched into church, one wonders what they will do when they get there. Obviously they cannot worship, for worship by its very nature is an acknowledgment of the transcendence of God.

So far as I can discover, God's fullness is to be understood only in the orthodox faith. "For, behold, the kingdom of God is within you" (Luke 17:21), our Lord said, but he also said, "When ye pray, say, Our Father which art in heaven, Hallowed be thy name" (Luke 11:2). Throughout the Gospels, Jesus reveals a God who is both immanent and transcendent: a God who dwells within us, yet who is the ruler of the universe; a God who is our Father, yet who is to be glorified in us and worshiped by us.

Perhaps in our common disappointment that the gospel is not universally accepted, we should recall that apparently our Lord never expected it to be. It is true that he said, "Go ye into all the world, and preach the gospel" (Mark 16:15), but he also said that if it were not received to go on (Luke 9:5), preaching the same gospel, not changing it to make it more readily acceptable.

We err in assuming that, simply because in this secular time we are scientifically and intellectually inclined, we are, ipso facto, unable and unwilling to accept the orthodox faith. I can only say that from one end of this country to the other, I have heard the same cry. It is not "Rationalize," but "Our souls thirst."

Never was this more apparent than at a recent healing conference I attended, this time not as a participant but as a visitor. Programmed and geared to the intellectual, the speakers used the word *God* only once and the name of Jesus not at all. The group attending the conference was, to be sure, highly educated, but their flesh longed for God and they found themselves indeed in a dry land (Ps. 63:1). Thirsting for the living water, they eagerly held out their cups, only to have them filled with the dry stones of erudition.

All this is not to say that we should not use our minds. We recognize the danger of a faith that leads to the impoverishment and even the closing of the mind. It is through our intellects, guided by the Holy Spirit, that we discover God's plan for the world and uncover the knowledge waiting for us. We know that the faith demands the full use of our intellects, but we also know that, while scientific curiosity may be satisfied by thought, insight into Jesus depends on holy obedience.

There are great mysteries of the faith that the human mind cannot ever hope to comprehend. Among these are Holy Communion, intercessory prayer, and the healing ministry. But we do not need to understand—only to obey. Surely one of the greatest of all gifts, one for which most of us today must perpetually pray, is the ability to accept simply the marvelous simplicity of God.

Saint Paul was a brilliant and highly educated man. The truest indication of his intellectual prowess was his knowledge and constant reiteration that our faith "should not stand in the wisdom of men, but in the power of God" (1 Cor. 2:5). The early Christians did not attempt to fathom the unfathomable; they humbly yielded themselves to the Holy Spirit and lived in and by the Spirit's power. This was enough for them, and it must be enough for us.

The comfort of the Christian faith is inexpressible, but Christianity is not primarily for those who need a crutch; it is for those who want Christ and accept the responsibility as well as the privilege of receiving him. In one sense Christianity is the most personal of all religions; in another it is the least private and necessarily the most outgoing. We are our brother's keeper on a scale most of us have never considered.

The Christian faith is seriously challenged today. Yet, as our Lord said, "by their fruits ye shall know them" (Matt. 7:16). In the fullness of the historic faith, I have seen brokenness of all kinds healed: grief, resentment, hate, unbelief. I have seen cures of emotional disturbances, of mental diseases, and of virtually every known physical ailment. These cures were received in the holy name of Jesus and by the power of the Holy Spirit.

The Church Universal: Overcoming Barriers

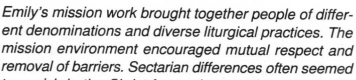

Emily's mission work brought together people of different denominations and diverse liturgical practices. The mission environment encouraged mutual respect and removal of barriers. Sectarian differences often seemed to vanish in the Christ-focused atmosphere. Believing firmly in the universality of Jesus' promises, Emily sought for ecumenical participation in all aspects of the healing ministry.

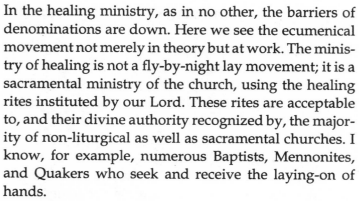

In the healing ministry, as in no other, the barriers of denominations are down. Here we see the ecumenical movement not merely in theory but at work. The ministry of healing is not a fly-by-night lay movement; it is a sacramental ministry of the church, using the healing rites instituted by our Lord. These rites are acceptable to, and their divine authority recognized by, the majority of non-liturgical as well as sacramental churches. I know, for example, numerous Baptists, Mennonites, and Quakers who seek and receive the laying-on of hands.

During the past three years I have noticed that the average number of denominations represented in a typical healing mission, even in a small church, is eleven. Behind one altar rail it is no longer uncommon to find a Lutheran pastor, a Methodist or Presbyterian minister, and an Episcopal priest—all ministering together to the kneeling supplicants of diverse parts of the church, united now by faith in the healing Christ.

More power is invariably manifested in interdenominational prayer groups; the same phenomenon occurs in healing services where there is participation by many denominations. I have observed this so often that it cannot be coincidence. It seems to me incontrovertible evidence of the power of God in the church universal.

Several years ago I was leading a mission in an Episcopal church where the laity had never been permitted to lay on hands behind the altar rail. During the first two days of the mission, this rule was enforced. However, since it is customary for the missioner to administer the healing rites, the congregation complained that I was not allowed to do so. The rector of the church finally asked me to participate with the clergy in the last two healing services.

The increased spiritual power was obvious to everyone in the church and, most of all, perhaps, to the rector. He and I discussed this phenomenon at some length after the mission. I remember offering a possible explanation that I have come to believe is fact: It was not I as an individual, but rather I as a lay person who was responsible for the increase of power, because I represented the entire laity, while he and the other participating ministers represented the entire clergy. Thus, between us, the whole mystical body of Christ was represented at the altar rail. Thence came the power.

I am so sure of this by now that, when I go to churches where only the missioner lays on hands, I plead for the participation of the clergy, in order to meet what I believe to be one of the necessary conditions for the maximum release of God's healing power.

In the ministry of healing is the closest approximation for many centuries to that oneness desired by our Lord (John 17:21); it is surely no accident that we recognize in this unity (which is his expressed holy will) so unmistakably the power of the risen Christ.

As the effectiveness of the healing ministry is enhanced by its universality, so its ecumenical viewpoint is fostered by this ministry's ability to enable us to respond to and benefit from one another's way of worship. A good example comes from a recent mission in an Episcopal church. In addition to the usual denominations represented at the mission was a group of Pentecostals from a nearby Church of God. After one of the healing services, I was in the sacristy waiting for the last person to leave before going back to my hotel. Believing the church empty, I put on my coat. Then I heard sounds coming from the sanctuary. I looked out the sacristy door and saw in the process of kneeling some ten men and women, members of the Pentecostal group I had met the night before. One of them caught my eye and beckoned me to come out. When I did so, he rose and said quietly, "We came up here to offer praise and thanksgiving for the healings that took place here tonight. Will you lead us in prayer?"

I did so with joy, beginning with spontaneous prayer. Then I suddenly felt impelled to end with the Divine Praises, which I asked the group to repeat after me phrase by phrase. The sound of those Spirit-filled voices repeating the opening *Blessed be God, Blessed be His Holy Name* is still with me. It was an extraordinarily moving act of devotion. The presence of God was almost palpable. That night, in a different and totally unplanned way, the oneness of the mystical body was again evidenced. The spontaneous and informal prayer, coupled with a traditional prayer of praise, resulted in a singularly complete offering of praise and thanksgiving.

In the liturgical churches all over the nation, I feel a new spirit and a new life of evangelism; in the non-sacramental churches, I discern a new understanding of, and a great hunger for, the sacraments. The healing ministry is a catalyst and a ministry of reconciliation.

Not long ago, I led a mission in a large Presbyterian church. Present at every service, including all the prayer group meetings, was a distinguished white-haired gentleman. At the end of the three-day mission, he spoke to me for the first time. He introduced him-self—a retired Baptist missionary, eighty-five years old. He shook my hand and exclaimed, "Praise the Lord! I haven't heard the gospel preached like this in fifty years!" Then, face aglow, he said with a smile, "Now I can die happy." This elderly man of God could say that, despite the strong sacramental emphasis of all my talks.

A question often arises about the relationship between the Jewish faith and spiritual healing. The Jews practice no healing ministry as such, although a number of rabbis have told me of healings among their people resulting from prayer. God healed long before the Word was made flesh and continues to heal today, though the Word may go unrecognized. However, the healing ministry is a Christian ministry. Because through Jesus healing power was given to the church, we ask for healing in his name.

Many Jews attend healing services and, to the best of my knowledge, no Christian clergy have refused to administer the healing rites to them. At one time I doubted both the propriety and the efficacy of this, but a personal experience in the recent past caused me to rethink the matter.

It was late one Friday evening when I received a telephone call from a stranger. She told me in a choked voice that her ten-year-old daughter had been sent home from the hospital to die and asked me if I would go to see the child. When I said that I would go on Sunday, the mother replied that this would in all probability be too late. The little girl was not expected to live over the weekend.

I readily agreed to go at once and was about to hang up when my caller said, "I guess I should tell you that we are of the Jewish faith." Under the circumstances I could only say, "Do you know that the healing ministry is a Christian ministry?" She replied, "Yes, I know. But please, please come."

Thus personally confronted with the actual situation, I understood how one could not refuse to minister, especially where a child was concerned. I knew the danger. This had been a call of sheer desperation; the family knew little or nothing of the healing ministry and undoubtedly had it confused with magic. Nevertheless, I had to go.

I prayed fervently in the car that the Holy Spirit would put the right words in my mouth. While I knew that I could not deny my Lord, neither could I upset the faith of a desperately sick child.

God took over the situation from the moment I entered the house. I found the parents to be deeply religious people and ascertained that their daughter had been taught of the historical Jesus. I spoke to the little girl about Jesus, telling her of his earthly ministry and how God, through him, healed the sick. I told her how he prayed and laid on hands, that today we use the same prayer, and that God still heals. I told her I would like to pray that way for her because she was sick and because God loved her and wanted her to be well again. She smiled and nodded.

Before administering the healing rites, I knelt briefly for the consecration of my hands, praying as usual in the Name of the Holy Trinity. Then, the mother and father standing at the foot of the bed, I laid on hands and silently said the healing prayer, using aloud only the word "Lord."

Great power was released, and I let my hands remain on her head for several minutes. Just as I removed them, I heard her whisper, "Thank you, Lord Jesus." I knew then that he had entered the heart of a little child, who had recognized him and called him by name. I knelt in a silent prayer of praise and thanksgiving.

The healing ministry bridges all manner of differences, as Emily later noted, not only those that arise in the divided church but also the simple, personal differences among human beings, differences that we attribute to heredity, environment—and the glorious fact of each person's uniqueness in the eyes of God.

The faith and some of the great leaders of faith make clear the wide diversity of temperament among Christians throughout the ages. There is no characteristically Christian disposition or personality. Jesus ministered to people of every conceivable background, and he used a variety of methods.

He healed frequently by touch, as in the case of the widow of Nain's son (Luke 7:11-15); and by word, as with the centurion's servant (Luke 7:1-10). He healed by intercession, as in the Syrophoenician woman's daughter (Matt. 15:21-28), and by anointing a blind man (John 9:6). He healed through the forgiveness of sins, as in the case of the palsied man (Mark 2:3-12), and by exorcism, as with the mute demoniac (Matt. 9:32-33).

The healing power of God, then, is not restricted to any one church or human temperament or method of ministry. Nor is God's response to prayer limited to any one form of supplication. This was beautifully illustrated during a recent mission. An extremely ill Episcopal priest was in attendance. After one of the services, he sent word that he wanted to see me. As we talked, it was clear that he was a strict Anglo-Catholic, and I realized that it was difficult for him to come to me, a woman, for help. I also realized how difficult it would be for him to receive a sacramental rite from a laywoman.

When it came time for the laying-on of hands and healing prayer, I sensed intuitively that this very Catholic, older priest would feel more comfortable if some of his fellow clergy were to participate. I asked him if he would like me to go back into the church and gather together any priests I could find. He nodded, so I did just this, managing to locate four. We all laid hands on the sick man together, while I prayed the healing prayer. But it was not I who prayed, it was the Holy

Spirit, who knew far better than I how best to meet this man's need. I suddenly found myself on my knees and heard myself saying some of the great liturgical prayers that I didn't even realize I knew from memory. They were prayers this priest loved and understood, and through them God worked to bless and heal.

The other priests joined with me as the prayers were concluded with the Sanctus from the Episcopal service of Holy Communion. Tears of peace and joy streamed down the sick man's face.

Immediately following this episode, a Pentecostal Christian came to talk with me about his problem. Obviously his prayer need could not be met with liturgical prayers from the Episcopal Book of Common Prayer. For him, the Holy Spirit prayed in me in an entirely different way, this time pleading the blood of Jesus. This prayer the supplicant understood, and was blessed by God through it.

God meets the need wherever it is, and the Holy Spirit intercedes according to his will (Rom. 8:27). Thus the prayer requirement, whatever the background or temperament of the supplicant, is met.

The Sacrament of Wholeness

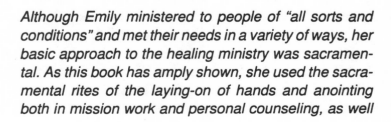

Although Emily ministered to people of "all sorts and conditions" and met their needs in a variety of ways, her basic approach to the healing ministry was sacramental. As this book has amply shown, she used the sacramental rites of the laying-on of hands and anointing both in mission work and personal counseling, as well

*as in formal liturgical services. We have just read of her
enthusiasm for variety in the approach to healing, for
freedom to adjust to differences in doctrine and temperament, and for openness to the leading of the Holy
Spirit. To place this in balance, however, we should
consider also her often-stated conviction that the Holy
Eucharist is "the greatest of all healing services."*

◆

Holy Communion is the ultimate means of sacramental
grace and the greatest of all God's gifts. I find it to be, as
Saint Thomas has said, the consummation of the spiritual life. Each of the sacraments gives us a special grace,
a part of the love of God, but in the Eucharist we find all
the fullness of God's love and power. It is for us the culmination of the entire faith and the climax of our personal relationship with Christ. We find in it all theology
and all doctrine, all the benefits of the Incarnation and
the Passion, all reconciliation and healing. In fact, we
find Christ himself.

"Surely Christ is not to be found or known only
through Holy Communion!" you may say, and of
course you are right. He is found and experienced, revealed and known, in many ways, especially through
prayer and Scripture. Christ is received, however, in
the Holy Eucharist, which was instituted for that purpose. He is always present and always accessible, but
in Holy Communion we enter into a unique relationship with him, a union not possible for many of us in
any other way.

Regardless of our church affiliation or sacramental
emphasis or interpretation, we cannot deny the healing

power in the Eucharist. In baptism we are regenerated by the Holy Spirit, often physically as well as spiritually; in Holy Communion, if we receive by faith the body and blood of our Lord, not only our spirits but frequently our bodies are made whole. This is a fact the ancient church knew well. For centuries, healing was closely associated with the sacrament, and the primitive liturgies of the church continually emphasized total salvation, the saving of both the soul and body. In the great eucharistic prayer of the ancient Liturgy of Saint Mark we find: "O Physician of souls and bodies, overseer of all flesh, oversee and heal us by thy salvation"; in the Liturgy of Saint John Chrysostom: "Heal the sick, O physician of our souls and bodies. . . ."

As many of us in the healing ministry view the sacraments with new eyes, we notice, for perhaps the first time, that in the Order for Holy Communion in the Book of Common Prayer, there are many references to bodily healing, culminating in the words of administration: "The Body of our Lord Jesus Christ, which was given for thee, preserve thy body and soul. . . ."

This uniting of the physical with the spiritual is uniquely Christian. Throughout his earthly ministry, Jesus demonstrated his concern for the bodily as well as the spiritual needs of people. He fed hungry bodies as well as hungry souls; he healed sick bodies as well as sick spirits. Jesus teaches that the complete person consists of body as well as soul—both now and in the life to come. This is the Christian doctrine of immortality, the doctrine of eternal life in which we already live.

In Holy Communion, sacramentally present, Jesus brings himself and the entirety of his life to his people. He exists whether or not we confess him, his presence is real whether or not we recognize it, and his healing power resides in his body and blood, whether or not we acknowledge it. When we do acknowledge it and receive the sacrament by faith with thanksgiving and expectancy, our lives are inevitably transformed: Since the Eucharist is the sacrament of wholeness, we are frequently physically healed.

In Holy Communion we experience most vividly the mystery of eternity, where past, present, and future are simultaneous. We are redeemed, yet still in the process of redemption; the sacrifice was offered once for all, yet is offered daily at God's altars, where the living Christ makes each one of us a part of his passion. The sacrifice is continuing and perpetual, just as we were saved two thousand years ago and are still in the process of being saved. It is only in this sense of the "going on-ness" of the sacrifice that we can even begin to understand the devastating character of sin. The appalling realization that our sins crucified Jesus, that they continue to crucify him, supplies the strongest motivation for our struggle toward holiness.

The greatest of all acts of love, the Eucharist, is also the sacrament of mystical exchange. It is the actualization of Christ's love of us, of the love of the Father for him, and of the love with which we are to love one another: the means through which we can best express our love for him. As Christ comes to us, we come to him, offering our lives—our bodies, our minds, our hearts, our souls as "a living sacrifice, holy, acceptable unto God" (Rom. 12:1).

In the unstinted giving of ourselves, we find that Christ has given us himself. In our self-emptying, we are filled with him. When this happens, we realize the dynamics of the Eucharist: As Christ has long known us, so at last our eyes are opened and we know him (Luke 24:31). At this moment of recognition, he becomes the supreme reality of our lives.

The Eucharist is a corporate act, but at the same time it meets our deepest individual needs. To be sure, it is above all an act of adoration and worship and thanksgiving, yet contained within it is every kind of prayer. At a recent gathering, I mentioned receiving Holy Communion with "special intention." As I spoke, a man in the group began to frown, and when I finished, he said, "I just don't get this. If the Eucharist is primarily an act of worship, why not for once just worship and not ask for anything? We can do this in our private prayers."

Yes, and we should. Holy Communion, however, is the most powerful means of intercession. At every Eucharist, Christ's perfect sacrifice for the salvation of the world is offered. As it is offered for the world, it is fitting to include prayers for God's blessing upon causes within the world, such as peace, missions, the unity of the church, and even the church supper taking place tonight. As it is offered for every soul in the world, it is fitting to offer Christ's sacrifice on behalf of anyone who may be sick or unhappy or in trouble. I firmly believe this constitutes the most powerful act of intercession available to us.

In this great corporate act of worship, we are part of the offering of countless churches and their people throughout the world. Each one of us constitutes a single link in an endless chain—an unexpendable link, if the full strength of the chain is to be realized. In the Eucharist, as in no other worship and in no other way, it is clear that no Christian ever prays alone, for we pray with the whole New Testament church, in the company of all faithful people, living and dead. In the sacrament of consummation, as the Eucharist was called in the ancient church, heaven and earth become mysteriously one.

In the following excerpts Emily writes further on the meaning of the Eucharist and the practice of making a spiritual communion. She addresses our need for thoughtful preparation to receive, and the frequent emergence of a longing to give.

The Eucharist is a holy mystery. No one really understands its full meaning. However, its transforming power we know well. It is my conviction that no one who has the remotest idea of what he is doing can receive the body and blood of Christ and remain unchanged.

Many churches regard Holy Communion as merely a memorial: "Do this in *remembrance* of me." One difficulty lies in the translation of the Greek word *anamnesis*. It has the sense of recalling, reenacting, having an immediate effect on an event. Thus, "Do this in remembrance of me," does not imply a looking back into the past, but rather the bringing of the past into the present.

Obviously those who hold a different view of Holy Communion are not denied healing. God is in no way bound by the sacraments (although I undoubtedly am!).

If you are unable, for reasons beyond your control, to receive Holy Communion as often as you would like, you may make a spiritual communion. At whatever time of day or night you do this, you will know that at that moment there will be churches somewhere in the world offering the Eucharist at their altars. Thus, in union with the faithful, offer Christ your sacrifice of praise and thanksgiving, seek the forgiveness of your sins, and pray this prayer of Saint Therese Couderc: "Lord Jesus, I unite myself to your perpetual, unceasing, universal sacrifice. I offer myself to you every day of my life and every moment of every day." (T88)

As the presence of Jesus is real whether or not human minds recognize it, so is his healing power residual in the body and blood whether or not we acknowledge it or are in a state to receive it. Receptiveness can be dramatically increased by the grace of God, if we follow as best we can the adjurement of Saint Paul to examine ourselves carefully before we "eat of that bread, and drink of that cup" (1 Cor. 11:28). He tells us that if we fail to *prepare* ourselves, we eat and drink unworthily.

As St. Paul appears to associate "unworthiness" chiefly with lack of self-examination, the remedy becomes crystal clear. Few of us partake of the sacrament irreverently. Few would receive it sacrilegiously, although carelessness and indifference constitute an unintentional desecration. Yet how many of us receive it unworthily simply because of lack of preparation. I mourn those lost years of self-privation when, in my carelessness, I never took time out to prepare myself in any way for what now seems to me God's greatest gift.

Receive it fasting, as did the early Christians, that you may be spiritually sensitized to Christ's presence in all its fullness. Receive it expectantly, as did the early Christians, so that you may know, perhaps for the first time, what Saint Paul really meant when he said: "The Christ is a tremendous power within you" (2 Cor. 12:9).

I have spoken only of what we receive from the sacrament of Holy Communion, and I must admit that for a long time this was my sole consideration. But I have found that as through the healing ministry we learn to know God better and to love him more, many of us reach the point when coupled with our ever-present desire to receive, is an overwhelming longing to *give*.

"This have I done for thee. What hast thou done for Me?" This question rings in our minds and echoes in our hearts, finally demanding an answer. The answer for me, and I know for many, has been found in the sacrificial Eucharist, which offers us a unique and wonderful means by which we can present to God ourselves, the offering that is the best we know to give.

While, of course, it is true that we may offer ourselves in every aspect of our daily lives and in all our human contacts, yet it is a deep psychological need as well as a human desire to give a distinctly *personal* gift to the loved one—a gift specifically of and from ourselves. It is through this holy sacrament of mystical exchange that we may give ourselves to Christ. We pray with Saint Ignatius of Loyola: "Take, O Lord, and receive my entire liberty, my memory, my understanding, and my whole will. All that I am, all that I have, thou hast given me, and I will give it back again to thee to be disposed of according to thy good pleasure."

No one who believes in the healing Christ need be deprived of the benefits of the healing ministry. Although there are many churches that have not as yet instituted specific healing ministries, almost every Christian church offers Holy Communion. Make this, then, *your* healing service, partaking as often as you can. As your understanding of this sacrament grows, as by God's grace and your own meticulous self-examination you receive it "worthily," your receptivity will increase until you are able to experience the power inherent in this greatest of all healing sacraments. (H154)

Christian Healing and Medical Practice

——————◆——————

A matter of basic concern in the healing ministry is its relationship to the practice of medicine. In introducing the healing ministry to her readers and those who attended her missions, Emily always established early her strong belief that the church's ministry of healing should be performed in cooperation with, and not instead of, or in opposition to, the practice of medicine.

Her interest in contemporary trends in medicine continued throughout her life. In the late 1980s she preached on the findings of Norman Cousins as set forth in Anatomy of an Illness, *and watched with interest his follow-up work at the University of California Medical Center, described in his later books. She spoke of the books of Dr. Bernard Siegel, a noted surgeon who writes of exceptional patients and their attitudes, as being "deeply spiritual." Always looking for new modes of cooperation between clergy and medical caregivers, she would have welcomed the current advances in mind/body research.*

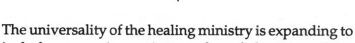

The universality of the healing ministry is expanding to include an ever-increasing number of physicians. During many missions, I have been privileged to meet with groups of medical doctors. Each time I have observed much the same pattern.

There is an initial hostility, because the doctors identify the church's ministry of healing with those sects that discourage medical treatment or with unscrupulous tent evangelists who exhort their people to throw out their drugs and discard their crutches. However, when physicians come to understand the spiritual emphasis of the healing ministry, I find them almost invariably sympathetic.

In addition to the misunderstandings of many doctors about the attitude of this ministry toward medicine, there is the misunderstanding of a few over-zealous laity who feel that to consult a physician shows a lack of faith in God. Most people who work in the healing ministry emphasize the fact that God mediates healing through various channels, which most certainly include medicine. God works through physicians, and those who need healing should seek it through both medicine and religion.

Nevertheless, no matter how much this fact is stressed, there are always some like the woman who called me late one night several months ago, a sixty-eight-year-old woman whom I have never met. For more than a year she called me approximately every six weeks to ask for prayer for a painful back condition that was not responding to medical treatment. In her most recent call, she asked again for prayer because she had a severe hemorrhage. I agreed to her request, suggested she attend a local healing service if possible, and urged her to see her doctor first thing in the morning. Her immediate response to the last suggestion was, "No, I wouldn't think of it. That would show a terrible lack of faith."

I explained to her then what I strongly believe. In my opinion, it is actually a sin not to consult a physician under such circumstances. God *is*, not merely *has*, knowledge, and God works through human beings. To reject medical knowledge is, therefore, to reject God. Moreover, in an attitude like hers, there seem to be strong elements of pride and presumption. She is demanding that God heal her in accordance with her wishes. She demands the direct intervention of the Holy Spirit, rather than leaving the method of healing in God's hands. People adopting this attitude usually do grave harm to themselves and, inadvertently, to the healing ministry.

When doctors understand the true nature of spiritual healing, they are eager to have the cooperation of clergy, who know their task is to help the sick (and not just to pray), console the dying, and administer last rites. When physicians observe the results of the healing ministry among their patients, they are very often more ardent promulgators of this ministry than the clergy.

I remember well a group of physicians to whom I spoke during a recent mission. Before I finished my last sentence, a hand shot up. I nodded, and the doctor asked, "How can I bring my patients to believe in the healing Christ?"

His interest, like that of a number of physicians, had been triggered by the medically inexplicable recovery of a patient. Unfortunately, at that time there was not a minister in town who conducted healing services.

At the same meeting, another doctor told about the healing of his own child. She had suffered from an allergic condition so severe that, on more than one occasion, her life had been in jeopardy. In the middle of an attack, she had received the laying-on of hands with prayer from a visiting missioner. The symptoms immediately subsided, and there had been no recurrence for over three years. "When this happens so close to home," said the physician, a former skeptic, "you just can't deny it. You have to believe."

A few days ago, I heard a similar viewpoint expressed, one I hear more and more frequently. I was speaking to a gathering of prayer groups, and in the audience was the wife of the town's leading pediatrician. At the conclusion of the meeting the pediatrician called to take her home, and she introduced me to her physician-husband. His opening remark was, "You may be interested to hear that one of the first things I do when I have a very sick child is to give his name to my wife's prayer group. These babies always seem to get well." Then he added, "I'll admit I used to think the healing ministry was complete bunk, but I've sure learned better over the past three years!"

Many doctors, like these I have mentioned, have come to believe in the healing ministry because of the surprising healings they have seen when prayer was offered. They have come to acknowledge a correlation between the healing and prayer. Others—and I know several—have come to believe because they have received healing. However, I believe that the majority of doctors come to acknowledge the validity of this ministry because they have witnessed the extraordinary triumph with which the dying faithful face death.

Such a case is that of a man critically ill who was on fire with faith in the living, healing Christ. Upon his admittance to the hospital, he suggested to the attending physician that the hospital make available to every patient some pamphlets explaining the ministry of healing, a list of healing ministers, and a list of books dealing with spiritual healing. The physician, totally unfamiliar with the subject, quite understandably pooh-poohed the whole matter.

The sick man died, but the physician's reaction was not "I told you so." Profoundly impressed with the spiritual stature of his patient and the way both he and his family met death, the doctor looked into the healing ministry. The result of his investigation is that he has now made available in his own office the same material recommended by his former hospital patient. The last time I spoke with this doctor, he made an astute observation: The healing ministry emphasizes wholeness of the body and the mind as well as of the spirit, but at the same time, it prepares for death by removing all fear of death.

One of the nation's leading hematologists has listed those illnesses that possibly originate in the emotions, where spiritual elements may well be involved. Among the many ailments which may be peculiarly responsive to spiritual as well as medical care are migraine headaches, epilepsy, ulcers, canker sores, eczema, psoriasis, cardiovascular disease, arthritis, and allergies. In the case of allergy, he notes that unconscious patients do not go into shock from horse serum, however allergic they may be to it when conscious.

As more and more diseases are discovered to be, at least in part, psychosomatic, it becomes increasingly clear that physical disease is a process and not an entity, a manifestation of something wrong, but not the wrong itself. This realization creates an increasing tendency in many conservative Christian doctors to admit that spiritual forces are involved in the successful treatment of illness. As the healing ministry spreads, there is growing cooperation between physicians and clergy, both in and outside of hospitals.

Some months ago I spoke at Bellevue Hospital in New York and saw an example of such cooperation in action. In this hospital the chaplains routinely lay hands on patients for healing, and each patient who is to undergo surgery is accompanied to the operating room by a minister who believes in the will and in the power of God to heal. Sometimes, at the request of the operating surgeon, the minister remains in the operating room to pray both for the guidance of the physician and for the healing of the patient.

For many years the medical profession as a whole has adhered strongly to the philosophical doctrine that asserts the essential distinction between body and soul. This body-soul dualism is one of the most ancient philosophical issues. Most theologians, led by Saint Paul, have long recognized that each of us is a single being, with body, mind, and spirit overlapping and interrelated. Today, many physicians acknowledge the validity of this viewpoint.

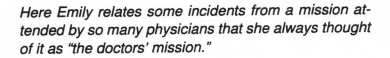

Here Emily relates some incidents from a mission attended by so many physicians that she always thought of it as "the doctors' mission."

Arriving the day before the mission was to begin, I had a long talk with the rector of the church. He told me that not only did the people in his locality know virtually nothing of the ministry of healing, but they were strongly prejudiced against it. It seems their sole contact with the ministry had been via television evangelists whose methods they cordially disliked. The reason the pastor had been anxious for my mission, he said, was that people might learn the difference between revivalist ministries (of which some are excellent, incidentally) and the sacramental ministry of the church. The problem was to get people to come and see. I did a lot of praying that afternoon, and was delighted that night to find the church well-filled, though far from overflowing.

At the end of the first service, people spoke to me rather diffidently. A few said in very low tones, as if afraid they might be overheard, "I think maybe I was healed tonight." One woman, however, had the courage of her convictions, and said loudly, "Praise God! I was totally deaf and now I can hear." As she went out the door, she flung over her shoulder, "My husband is an ear specialist. I can't wait to tell him what happened!" (He came the following night to see what was "going on in that church.")

After everyone had left, I turned to walk back to the sacristy when someone called my name. As I turned back, a well-dressed, attractive man in his mid-forties came up to me and said urgently, "Could you have supper with me tonight? I understand you don't dine before the service." I hesitated a moment and he said, "Please. It's important." I looked at the pastor of the church, standing a few feet away. He nodded, "It's all right. He's a member of the church."

He had a very bad back, he told me, so bad that he was contemplating giving up his medical practice. When it came time for the laying-on of hands, he rebelled. He stood up to let others go past him, and then quickly decided to take this opportunity to escape! As the others went up to the altar rail, he planned to sneak out the front door of the church. But everyone in the church was moving forward, and he found he could not "navigate against the traffic." Thus, unable to walk in the opposite direction, he was swept along with the others. He said, "I had to stand until I thought I would die, and then at last I found myself at the altar rail." As everyone else was kneeling, and he did not want to appear conspicuous, he painfully got to his knees, finding himself so hemmed in that he was forced to kneel upright with his hands at his side instead of on the rail. "With even more strain on my back," he continued, "I figured right then that this healing mission would put me in the hospital."

Finally it was his turn to receive the laying-on of hands, and with a sigh of relief, he carefully arose, and was halfway back to his pew before he realized that his back was not hurting. "For the first time in four years," he told me jubilantly, "I am without pain," whereupon he leapt to his feet in the restaurant and touched his toes with the palms of his hands. He attended every session of the mission thereafter and made a wonderful witness as a formerly unbelieving doctor.

The final day was the clergy and doctor luncheon. For the first time in my experience, there were many more physicians there than clergy. At the time for questions, one of the doctors raised his hand and said, "I would like to know how to bring my patients to believe in the healing Christ." At this a chorus joined in, "I want to know the same thing." Then one of the physicians made a remark that amused me. "Where are the clergy in this? Like all of my fellow doctors, I'm terribly busy. It's all I can do to handle my practice. I just wish the clergy would do their share, and not leave the 'converting' to us." Very true, but let it be said that in most places the clergy *do* do their share! (T148)

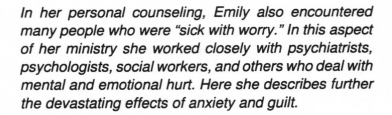

In her personal counseling, Emily also encountered many people who were "sick with worry." In this aspect of her ministry she worked closely with psychiatrists, psychologists, social workers, and others who deal with mental and emotional hurt. Here she describes further the devastating effects of anxiety and guilt.

Many psychiatrists and psychologists claim that the two overriding existential anxieties are *guilt* and *fear of death*, and my own experience, however limited, confirms this claim. The majority of disturbed people voice a common complaint and share a common problem: They are beset by feelings of guilt, and they are unable to accept the forgiveness of God. I have come to believe that this inability often has one primary source: the patient's lack of conviction of God's love.

I have seen the devastation wrought by feelings of unrelieved guilt, a devastation which often begins with a mild sense of "wrongness" and evolves into increasing unhappiness until in some cases it climaxes in contemplated suicide.

A desperate woman came to me late one night, threatening to kill herself. Most potential suicides need psychiatric help, and it is my custom to refer them to someone better qualified than I. However, this woman had insisted over the telephone that she see me first, and at once. Like others with the same problem, she called me because she was a religious person. Therefore, she was receptive to a direct religious approach.

After talking for two hours about the problems that made her life unendurable, she finally came to the real problem. She had committed a serious sin several years before, and her feeling of guilt had grown until, overwhelmed with despair, she couldn't live with it any longer.

"But killing yourself won't solve your problem," I interjected. "It will still be waiting for you afterwards." She looked startled, and I prayed for guidance to say something that would reach her. "You said you were a Christian?" I asked. She nodded. "Then," I said, "you must know that the life we live here is a part of the life eternal, that your life will go on, whether or not in this world."

I went on to say what I firmly believe: God gives

each of us time on this earth to become holy by grace. To cut this time short by our own hand requires that the portion of the road to sanctity that we fail to tread here be resumed on the other side, at the precise point at which we voluntarily and in our right mind left it.

She thought this over and then asked, "How can I 'become holy,' as you say, when I've already committed so terrible a sin I can't even forgive myself?"

"But God can forgive you," I replied. "All you have to do is believe this, and to ask. Don't limit God's capacity for forgiveness by your own incapacity." She looked at me and said dubiously, "But surely even God can't forgive this."

The way was now open to explain to her, gently but firmly, that her greatest sin was not in what she had done, but in her present attitude of pride. "What's so special about your sin," I asked, "that makes it greater than the sins of anyone else?" She did not answer. I assured the woman that, no matter how great the sin that may torture our conscience, no sinner is beyond the love of God. Nothing can separate us from this love except our lack of penitence. The only way we can alienate ourselves from God's love is by an act of the will in which we deliberately continue to choose evil.

As I spoke, I saw the expression in her eyes change. When I added that repentance, too, is an act of the will, and that from the instant we even wish to make an act of contrition, it is in a sense already made in the eyes of God, I saw her burden discernibly ease.

Before the night was out, that woman was kneeling with me, pouring out her confession to God and asking forgiveness. To give God's absolution reality to her, I asked her to say aloud, "In the name of Jesus Christ I have been forgiven." She did this, and rose from her knees with tears of joy streaming down her face. For the first time in five years she felt clean and truly absolved. Her offering had been "a broken and a contrite heart" and God had not despised it (Ps. 51:17).

I suggested to her that if she felt threatened again by feelings of guilt, she should repeat the same vocal affirmation. She followed this advice, and has now learned well that the God of love is not so quick to anger as she had believed, nor so reluctant to forgive as she had thought.

An almost invariable component of guilt is self-abasement. So it was with a woman who came to see me not long ago. She complained of a number of physical ailments that had no apparent medical cause. In addition to these, she was plagued by a continual feeling of guilt over nothing in particular and everything in general. After hearing her say repeatedly, "I hate myself" and in the same breath speak of "loving God," I interposed the thought that she was stating an impossible contradiction. Since she was made and loved by God, to hate herself meant to hate God's creation and certainly not to love the Creator.

On the first visit I detected in her an almost masochistic pleasure in her violent self-denunciation. With calculated forethought, I decided not to mince words. "Calvary proved how much God loves you," I said, "and you are now questioning the worth of Christ's sacrifice. How dare you hate yourself when Christ loved you enough to die for you?" Watching her face closely, I decided it was safe to add, "Your presumption is the real sin."

These remarks served their intended purpose; they

started a new train of thought. Before she left, and at her request, we prayed together that she might really know the love of God. She got up from her knees with shining eyes. However, the problem of her vague and gnawing feeling of guilt still remained.

On the next visit, I questioned her briefly about her childhood. She told me, as have so many, that she remembered that, when she was a little girl, she often felt guilty, even when she had done nothing wrong. As I listened to this woman I wondered, as I have wondered before in cases of this kind, if her vague sense of guilt were not perhaps an infantile carryover into adult life, where the fear of losing the love of a parent is transferred to a fear of losing the love of God. Knowing that a sense of security is often restored by drawing an analogy between human love and the love of God, I asked her if she loved her children. At her quick affirmation, I said, "Do you love them only when they are good?"

She shook her head and said with a smile, "Hardly! If that were so, I wouldn't love them most of the time!" And so, I assured her, it was with God, who loves us because we are his children, not because we are good.

During subsequent visits, we talked mostly about how wonderful a thing the love of God is: how in infinite compassion, God stands always not only ready, but longing to forgive, if we will only ask. At the end of our last visit, the woman knelt and committed her life to Christ. She is a totally changed person. Free of all physical symptoms, she is now a devout believer and an active, valuable member of a prayer group.

The consensus of psychologists is that real guilt can usually be handled satisfactorily by pastoral counseling or confession; but if guilt is imagined, it usually requires psychotherapy. This is a safe yardstick, although not invariably reliable. Even the most competent psychotherapist cannot by means of psychotherapy grant absolution. A chaplain in a psychiatric hospital tells me that, every time he walks into the hospital, at least one physician asks him to visit a patient who suffers from guilt that the psychiatrist can not alleviate. "This is your job," the doctor says, "Teach him about the forgiveness of God." Here we see the ideal cooperation of religion and medicine that constitutes the total healing ministry.

CHAPTER SIX

Suffering and Joy
The Paradoxical Relationship

---◆---

In 1965 Emily undertook yet another major commitment of time and energy. At the invitation of the rector and with permission of the bishop, she began to lead weekly healing services at Calvary Episcopal Church in Pittsburgh. Among her deepest lifelong hopes was that every Christian church of every denomination should offer a ministry of healing, making the sacramental healing rites available regularly. In the work at Calvary, she and the clergy and lay ministers demonstrated one way in which this could be done: through a liturgical service, held regularly and conducted in an atmosphere of expectancy and love.

Leadership of this weekly service, in which she usually delivered a homily, added to Emily's workload and led also to an increase in requests for counseling. All of this, with her writing and her thriving mission career, made up a full and rigorous working schedule. Then came an event that would test her faith and change her life: an accident that caused severe spinal injury. Her physical suffering was both immediate and prolonged. Suffering became one of the two principal themes of *her sixth book,* The Healing Power of Christ. *The other theme is joy, and in this chapter we see the mysterious compatibility of great suffering and Christian joy.*

Facing the Challenge: Seek God First

For years I felt presumptuous when from the pinnacle of my own extraordinarily good health I would say to the suffering, "Seek ye *first* the kingdom. You must seek God for himself and not just for healing. There lies your best hope of physical healing." I no longer feel presumptuous in saying these words, and I know their validity as I never fully understood before. I have had to apply them to myself, because for a period of nearly six years I was never a day without pain, and had it not been for the strength of Christ in which I walked and worked, I would have been totally incapacitated. Although for years there was no evidence of healing in my own body, I feel myself not less blessed, but more— for I have known God's grace in my life to an extent I never knew before, continually sustaining, enabling, and empowering.

While I no longer feel hesitant in asking the suffering to seek God first, I do not underestimate the difficulty of this undertaking. I realize that there are times when pain supersedes all else, but there are also times when the pain, no matter what the ailment, is less. God's mercy requires only a moment of complete relinquishment to work a miracle.

Some of my beloved friends, without whose prayers I could not have continued, have said to me in real distress, "But why should *you* have to suffer so?" Deeply grateful for their concern, I was nevertheless upset by this question. The answer seemed to me so clear: Why *not* I? Everyone on earth is subject to suffering, and why should I be immune? To be a Christian is not an insurance policy against the coming of disaster; it is assurance against being overcome by it—for no matter what happens to us, we hold in our hearts the joy of the Lord, a joy submerged at times by pain or adversity, but always deep within our beings. We may indeed suffer, but Christ was crucified and rose again. No matter what happens to us, we know that beyond the Cross lies the Resurrection. In this knowledge lies that joy that cannot be taken from us.

Acquaintance with Pain

Glancing at my watch, I noted that within half an hour the plane would be arriving at my destination—a city far from home—where I was to lead a three-day healing mission. The flight attendant was serving coffee to the passengers when the plane hit rough weather. I smiled to myself at the seemingly inevitable simultaneity of air pockets and coffee-serving. As the "Fasten Seat Belt" sign flashed on, I started to reach out for my cup but quickly changed my mind. The plane was pitching and plunging too much to risk a shower of hot coffee. The flight attendant, undaunted, walked past me, struggling to keep her balance.

As the plane hit another air pocket I tightened my seat belt, and at that moment a small child, sitting a few seats in front of me, escaped from his parents and began to run up the aisle. The plane gave a lurch and the child started to fall. Instinctively I twisted quickly in my seat to catch him. That sudden movement of my body, confined as it was by the seat belt, wrenched my back in such searing pain that I thought I would faint.

At the time of the initial injury to my back, six months earlier, I had had to cancel one mission, fortunately the last of that season and the first I had ever had to cancel. It had been a difficult summer of lying flat on my back for weeks on end, but by the grace of God I was up and around once more and had recently completed several missions. As I sat in my plane seat now in excruciating pain, I could only pray, "Lord, if I am to do this mission, you'll have to make it possible."

The plane landed, and with superhuman effort I got myself down the ramp where I was met by the smiling rector, who was full of plans for the mission beginning the next day. I said nothing about my back until we arrived at the hotel where I was to stay. Unable to get out of the car, I was forced to tell him what had happened.

I will long remember his kindness. Instead of being upset over the probable cancellation of the event planned two years before and widely publicized, his sole concern was for me. After a short prayer, he called a physician who, after a cursory examination, said that I must be hospitalized at once.

"But what about the mission?" I asked.

"Forget it," was the response. But this was an unrealistic order, for how could I "forget" it when I knew that busloads of people were arriving from far-distant points, hundreds would be bitterly disappointed, and there was no time to procure another missioner?

Early next morning while I was still groggy from Demerol, the physician and rector stopped by my hospital room. Before either could speak, I said, "I'll do the mission." The physician demurred but was understanding, albeit skeptical. "All right," he said, "if you think you can. But of course you'll have to return to the hospital immediately after each session. Have therapy as often as possible, and we'll try to keep you free from pain."

An hour before I was to leave for the church for the opening service that evening, three nurses came in to dress me. A back brace had been hastily fitted, and while one nurse was strapping me into it as I lay on the bed, another was pulling on my stockings. The third nurse stood by my head and said, "Mrs. Neal, please don't try it. You'll never make it."

I knew better than anyone that I could never make it on my own—but I also knew that I could "do all things through Christ which strengtheneth me" (Phil. 4:13).

When I was finally dressed but still lying flat, the physician came in with a packet of pain pills. "Take one of these now," he said, "and carry the others with you. You can sneak one into your mouth as you take a sip of water from the pulpit."

I refused the pills, afraid to take them lest they befuddle my mind, and the physician left the room. To my surprise and joy, the nurses stood around my bed, and one of them said, "We'd like to pray for you before you go." Deeply grateful and greatly strengthened, I managed to get off the bed, and I was taken to the church.

As I stepped into the pulpit, the first person I saw was the kind physician, who had taken time off to come to the service; he was waiting to catch me if I fell. However, stronger hands than his were to hold me up that night.

The church was packed, and only the rector and I were to administer the laying-on of hands. According to usual custom we divided the altar rail, he taking one half and I the other. The line of people streaming up to receive the healing rite seemed endless. Each time I finished my section of the rail, I turned toward the altar with the silent prayer, "Lord, let thy strength be made perfect in my weakness." Little did I know that night that this would be the burden of my prayer for years to come, as during mission after mission I could not under der my own power stand on my feet.

By the time the last group came up to receive the laying-on of hands, I had been standing for nearly four hours, and I could scarcely walk. Reaching down to hang on to the altar rail, I suddenly felt a firm hand under my left elbow and then an arm around my waist, which held me up straight and strong until the service was over.

Next morning the rector telephoned me at the hospital and I thanked him for supporting me at the rail the night before. With some embarrassment I felt compelled to add, "I certainly needed your help last evening, as I was about to collapse, but tonight could you please get us more clergy to help with the laying-on of hands? I managed last night because you held me up and I am grateful, but please don't do it again. It seems hardly suitable at a formal service to have you with your arm around me!"

There was a long silence at the other end of the telephone—and then, in a small voice, came his words: "Emily, I didn't touch you during that service. I was finished before you, and during the last fifteen minutes I was kneeling before the high altar."

Then I knew: Not only had Christ upheld me, he had quite literally held me up. And so it was to be in the years that lay ahead. At home I was unable to stand for the reading of a psalm, but during a mission I was on my feet for three or four hours at a time, solely in his strength.

During this mission there was a great outpouring of the Holy Spirit, and many healings were reported. The only obligation I could not fulfill was that of greeting people after the services. If the time between the various daytime sessions was short, the rector would take me to his study, where with the door locked I lay on the floor (my back needed a hard surface) until it was time for the next event. Again, little did I know that for months and years to come, I would have to rest on the floor of a clergy study. I am sure my record is unique in one respect at least: Never has anyone lain on the floors of so many pastors' studies!

The letters I received later, demonstrated once again how any and everything can be used for God's glory. Typical of these letters was one which read: "I was miserably ill last week—and then I remembered your doing that mission in the strength of Christ. What an inspiration, as through you we saw the living Christ sustain and enable. Suddenly my own sickness seemed very trivial, and God healed me in record time."

It was recalling letters like this that caused me to believe that for others as well as myself, the visible evidence of the enabling power of the Holy Spirit was as great a miracle as a physical healing.

Through it all—the long hours spent in bed lying perfectly flat, unable to read because holding even a paperback book caused painful strain on the back, and the months that ran into years during which I could be up only four hours at a time—I was to learn much by the teaching of the Spirit, much of prayer, and what it meant to be alone with God.

I was to learn what it was to be stripped of pride—often, between connecting planes, I would be forced to lie down in airport waiting rooms, and on many occasions, on the floor of the airport's ladies' lounge.

I was to learn patience—and this in itself was a minor miracle, for by temperament I am impatient, hard-driving, hard-working, and filled with energy.

I was to learn a new compassion for all who suffer, for one who has not suffered cannot possibly comprehend it.

I was to learn experientially the validity of what I have so long taught: that when one is healed in spirit, the healing of the body is no longer of primary importance. Thus when people would say accusingly, "Why don't you ever speak of your back?" I could honestly reply, "Why should I? It's not that important."

I was to learn over the years that it is by love that God works. Love is God's power to convert and change lives, to heal, and to mend all brokenness. God's love calls us to obedience and makes it our joy to obey, no matter how rough the road or difficult the way.

In the missions and healing services that followed her injury, Emily noted an increase in the number of healings related to spinal problems. One case, of a woman healed of crippling arthritis, was particularly interesting.

She had come to me for a private interview on the first day of the mission, bent double, walking with great difficulty with the aid of two canes. She was a woman of great faith, and at the end of our talk, I said, "In the name of Jesus, walk." Her back straightened, she handed me her canes, arose from her chair, and walked three times around the room. At first her steps were hesitant, then firm and sure. She came to all of the services, where she offered thanksgiving and prayed for others. Like the woman during our Lord's earthly ministry, she was permanently loosed from her infirmity.

Then there were multitudinous healings of ruptured discs and spinal ailments of various kinds. Curiously enough, these are a frequent occurrence at healing services ever since the original injury to my own spine. I have never before witnessed so many healings of spinal trouble as over the past six years.

After the first service, I slipped away unnoticed and knelt at the altar rail of the darkened and empty church, thanking God for the awesome power of the Holy Spirit. I offered once more my injured back to be used for God's glory. I prayed with all my heart that if because of my pain I were to be a more open channel for God's healing grace, I would be permitted to keep it.

I was to think often of this prayer in the months to come, as the power of the Spirit seemed greater than ever before. I was fully aware of that narrow line between a neurotic desire to suffer, which makes us impervious to the healing power of the resurrected Christ, and offering the suffering we have, at the same time praying that God's perfect will for wholeness be fulfilled in us. In the end I was satisfied that I was on the right side of the line. Hating pain of itself, I was not rejoicing in my infirmity because I then had more to offer God. I could not embrace the pain as pain—but I could embrace it as the cross by which I could share in Christ's death and thus in his resurrection. If, for reasons I did not understand, God was using this pain—perhaps to purge and cleanse me that I might be an increasingly open channel, perhaps to protect me from spiritual pride in order that I might be a better instrument—then I would gladly endure. For the reason for my being was that God might be glorified and manifested through me.

This is not to say that in the pain-filled years ahead I did not falter. I did. It is not to say that I was never discouraged or at times demoralized by pain. I was. It is merely to say that in God's mercy I never felt forsaken.

Delayed Healing: Redemptive Suffering

Why is it that most healings are gradual? Sometimes the reason is obvious. Here are a few possible reasons: There may be blocks within the individual, spiritual sins such as resentment or hostility, that impede the inflow of God's healing power. When such factors do not appear to exist, we must suppose that the delay in healing is due to a weakness of faith in the church as a whole. (This was the belief and the explanation of the ancient church when healings failed to occur.) Then there is the self-evident fact that none of us is Jesus Christ, and hence we are not the completely open channels for healing that he was. Finally, I am convinced there may be divine purpose in many delayed healings.

I think often of some of the instant and extremely dramatic healings I have witnessed: The man long paralyzed who walked; the woman instantly healed of skin cancer; the deaf man whose ears were opened. All failed to return to give thanks, and all of them promptly forgot or ignored the source of all healing. The spirits of these individuals were left untouched, and thus they were not healed in the way that matters most. They were not made whole, and it is wholeness we seek in the healing ministry. Consider the ten lepers, only one of whom returned to give thanks for his healing. It was to this one alone that our Lord said, "Thy faith hath made thee whole" (Luke 17:11-19).

While it is true that in many cases the healing of the spirit—the closer union with God, which is the primary purpose of the ministry of healing—*follows* a physical healing, in most cases the healing of the spirit comes first.

A typical example is the case of a woman suffering from a large ovarian tumor who attended a healing mission about a year ago. When she and I had a brief conference during the mission, I found her seething with jealousy, bitterness, and resentment. I explained to her that unless she was liberated from these destructive emotions, her chances of physical healing were slight indeed. Thus we made the burden of our prayer not the disappearance of her tumor by the intervention of the Holy Spirit, but the release of her spiritual sins that hindered the inflow of God's grace. A wonderful thing happened to this woman, as it has to so many others. She told me later that after the healing prayer that evening at the service, the power of God came down upon her so mightily that it went though her body like an electric current and continued to do so throughout the night. A letter from her not long ago said that since the last night of the mission she has lost all her resentment, that she has been steadily growing in the knowledge and love of God, and since that time, her tumor has shrunk slowly but surely, until a recent medical examination proved it to be nonexistent.

Remains of the growth were gradually eliminated by her system over a period of seven or eight months. All during these months this woman had engaged in a spiritual struggle. Because she had expected instant healing, regardless of what I had said about the necessity of being rid of her own spiritual impediments, the fact that the power of God had flowed so strongly through her body led her to think I had been mistaken—that she was indeed going to receive the instantaneous healing she sought. She reasoned that she would take care of the hatreds and resentments with which she was filled *after* her physical healing. But it didn't work that way. God's power going through her body was a signal that she would be healed when she met the requirements. I can only believe that it was God's purpose that her physical healing be delayed, so that when it came, she would be in every way whole.

In my own case, while I have been quickly healed of many ailments, the healing of my back has been torturously slow—but I believe that not one second of suffering has been wasted. This suffering was not the primary will of God, nor did God send it, but I am certain God has used my suffering for a holy purpose.

While we await the completion of a gradual healing, no suffering need ever be fruitless or unavailing. For while it is true we believe that disease is not of the kingdom of God, we also know that when we offer it, God sanctifies both it and the sufferer. Further, in a way we cannot pretend to understand but neither can we doubt, God will use our suffering on behalf of others if we will only ask. This is a powerful mode of intercession given us by God, and obviously recognized by Saint Francis de Sales, who stated that whenever he was in dire need of prayer he invariably called upon someone who was in pain.

It has long seemed to me that redemptive suffering is one of the most awe-inspiring of all God's miracles. The trouble is that it is so rare. But those who know the healing Christ, those who with the Christian's sure and certain hope await their healing, can at the same time suffer redemptively.

There is nothing either morbid or contradictory in the healing ministry if, when you are suffering in any way, you pray that God will enable you to accept your suffering gladly, uniting it with our Lord's own perfect sacrifice. If we suffer in union with Christ, we have the privilege of sharing in a special way in the whole redemptive process. There can be a unique joy in offering our suffering on behalf of someone else who is in need of prayer. We have our scriptural authority for this in Saint Paul's words: "It is now my happiness to suffer for you. This is my way of helping to complete, in my poor human flesh, the full tale of Christ's afflictions still to be endured, for the sake of his body which is the church" (Col. 1:24).

This is not to say that your suffering or mine has any *atoning* merit, for the atonement belongs to Christ alone. He made the one full, perfect, and sufficient sacrifice for the sins of the world. No one of us can add to that. However, our suffering *does* lead to the setting free of life to be imparted to others. The words "for the sake of his body which is the church" mean that there is no separation between helping Christ and helping the church—for union with Christ means union with all those who are in him.

Here we come to a great paradox. Accepting your suffering never means that you must not simultaneously seek to resist and overcome it. The paradox involved here can be reconciled only by the Holy Spirit. It is the Spirit who teaches us through Scripture and revelation that suffering from disease is an evil, and that no man may desire it for its own sake. And yet in offering it to God to be used on behalf of another it is redeemed and thus becomes creative and constructive.

How do you offer your suffering? By praying something like this: "Lord, I offer you my sins, my contrite heart, my suffering, my entire life, such as it is—to be used for your glory—and please use it on behalf of John, whose need is so great." If you so pray with your heart, God will use your offering as you ask.

I remember well the young woman who came to Calvary for the first time in a wheelchair, her face white and drawn, her body racked by the pain of cancer no drugs could alleviate. On that particular night I happened to speak of offering one's suffering on behalf of another. The following week the young woman was back again, this time her face radiant. She told me that she had "practiced" all the preceding week the things I had suggested. Not only was the friend for whom she offered her pain healed, but she herself had dramatically improved. "The thought that my suffering was not wasted," she said, "but used by God to help someone else, has made the difference. This knowledge is better than a shot of morphine in making my own pain endurable."

What happened in the case of this young woman happens to many. We offer our suffering in union with that of Jesus, and not only are those for whom we pray helped, but, unsought and unasked, our own pain is very frequently relieved. How this "works" is one of God's greatest mysteries—but that it does work in many cases is beyond any doubt.

Although Scripture tells us to rejoice when we partake of Christ's suffering, we should not seek pain. There is a great difference between deliberately afflicting our bodies so that we may have more to offer God and using the affliction we have. Throughout the day, when you offer your suffering on behalf of another in need, give thanks that God is using you as an instrument. Then await with confidence the fullness of God's healing power in your own life.

When night comes, remember these words of Saint Paul: "Never get tired of staying awake to pray for all the saints" (Eph. 6:18). If you are sleepless for any reason, this is good advice, easy to follow, and your very sleeplessness becomes one more thing you may gratefully offer. The curse of sleeplessness becomes a blessing if you use the long, still hours of the night not in cloying self-pity or restless tossing, but in prayer on behalf of others who lie awake. As you offer your sleeplessness "for all the saints," you can be assured, although you do not know precisely how or why, that your intercessions will have great power, bringing comfort and solace to people you may not even know.

Holiness and Wholeness

During a recent mission an eighteen-year-old boy planning to enter the ministry asked me, "If people are holy, do they get sick?" At first glance this question may appear naive, but actually it is extremely astute. I explained to this young man that no one on earth is immune from illness, that as long as there is evil in the world, there will be suffering, and there will be evil on earth as long as human beings inhabit it.

Even as I spoke, I realized that too many people, lacking an adequate understanding of the healing ministry, tend to equate holiness with physical wholeness. It is true that the words "holiness" and "wholeness" have a common root. Most certainly it is God's will that all of us be physically as well as spiritually whole; otherwise, over one-third of the gospel would not be devoted to our Lord's earthly healing ministry. However, God's perfect will is often circumvented by reasons beyond our individual control, such as the evil and unbelief of the world, of which we are all victims. That God's will is temporarily deflected does not mean that an individual who happens to be physically ill cannot be gloriously whole in Christ.

There are many people like a woman I know who, in her forties, is afflicted with a rare and devastating type of arthritis. She expectantly awaits her physical healing, but in the larger and most important sense she is even now whole in Christ. She dwells in him, and he in her. To enter her presence is for me a benediction, as it is for all who know her.

The young man went on: "If holiness does not assure physical well-being, why do you speak continually of growing in grace and holiness, of the need to establish a closer union with God, so that physical healing may occur?"

The reason for my emphasis on this closer relationship with God, which obviously must result in increasing holiness, is this: The master key to all healing is found in the words, "Seek ye first the kingdom of God." As Christians we do not seek physical health for health's sake; we are called to seek God for God's sake. It is when we seek God above all else that we can reasonably expect that "all these things"—such as healing—"shall be added unto you" (Matt. 6:33).

The equation of holiness with physical health is untenable and does a grave disservice to the sick. One of the cruelest axioms I know, frequently quoted in the healing ministry, is "There is no such thing as an incurable disease, only incurable persons." There is, to be sure, a half-truth here, for there are no incurable diseases in the sight of God. I have witnessed healings of virtually every disease known, many of them termed medically incurable. However, in the second part of the axiom, the clear—and mistaken—implication is that the *patient* is invariably responsible if healing fails to occur. This assumption is in direct opposition to the teaching of the ancient church, which did not ascribe such failure to the individual's lack of faith, but to the church's as a whole.

Those who are suffering illness have enough to contend with without adding an unjustifiable burden of *guilt*. It is a well-known fact that the sick frequently suffer from guilt feelings simply because they are sick. It is a peculiar psychological truth that non-Christians also harbor guilt feelings during an illness, possibly because they feel they are causing their families worry and expense. Perhaps the prevalence of guilt feelings during illness comes from the fact that buried deep in the unconscious of many individuals, Christian or not, is the erroneous idea, promulgated by the church for so many centuries, that God sends sickness as a punishment.

Christians who believe wholeheartedly in the healing Christ are prone to feel the guiltiest of all. Some of us who work in the healing ministry, including myself, must assume responsibility for at least part of the emotional suffering the believer too often endures. We state categorically—and correctly—that sickness is *not* the primary will of God. But there is danger in this teaching if we do not expand upon it. It is fatally easy for the sick to misunderstand, to wonder if, because they are ill, they are really in the will of God at all.

As one woman put it, "I have cancer, and I am seeking the healing power of God. However," she went on, "if God's will is complete wholeness of body, mind, and spirit, does the fact that I am now physically sick mean that I am not in his will?"

This woman was a committed Christian. Her concern was not motivated by fear of continued physical pain, but rather by her fear that if she were *not* healed it would mean she was outside the will of God.

After extensive and intensive counseling among such individuals, during which I was able, I believe successfully, to allay their fears, I felt greatly blessed that my own suffering was not compounded by feelings of guilt or confusion. I am now even more certain that whether sick or well, we are all safely held in the palm of God's hand. I can say with complete assurance that you are most certainly held by God if you are praying in faith for your total wholeness.

If many Christians suffer needless guilt over their ill-nesses, there are also many who, as they await their healing, may be enduring great physical pain. Many of us do not fear death, but only the suffering we may have to endure in the process of dying. I vividly recall a woman who came to me directly after receiving her physician's verdict that her entire body was riddled with cancer. She said, "I know that Christ will heal me—if not here on earth, then when I am wholly with him. The only thing I really fear is the suffering, for I know I don't bear pain well."

This woman suffered greatly, but I recall how often she received the laying-on of hands with prayer, and how often her pain was either marvelously diminished or entirely eliminated for increasingly long periods of time. This is the mercy of God.

None of us understands the mystery of pain, suffer-ing, and disease. Our Lord made no attempt to explain it. He simply healed, making crystal clear that disease was not of the kingdom of God. He has given us the means of grace to combat the enemy: Prayer, sacra-ment, and the healing rites. When we use these God-given means, we invariably receive either surcease from pain or the strength to withstand it—and very of-ten the gift of complete healing.

Joy, Rebirth, and the Gifts of the Spirit

———————◆———————

Emily turns now from the mystery of pain and suffering to her wonder at God's grace in bestowing the gift of

*Christian joy. The simultaneity of suffering and joy is dif-
ficult for many to understand, but the healing ministry,
she believes, provides hard evidence that this can and
does occur.*

*Emily also tells of that joyous experience, or, as it
sometimes happens, that series of experiences, referred to as being "born again." She then pays tribute to
the joy-filled contributions of the charismatic movement, while cautioning against distortion or abuse of
the Spirit's gifts.*

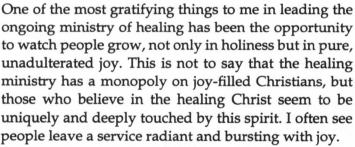

One of the most gratifying things to me in leading the
ongoing ministry of healing has been the opportunity
to watch people grow, not only in holiness but in pure,
unadulterated joy. This is not to say that the healing
ministry has a monopoly on joy-filled Christians, but
those who believe in the healing Christ seem to be
uniquely and deeply touched by this spirit. I often see
people leave a service radiant and bursting with joy.

This is the way it *should* be. A long face and mournful
demeanor are a travesty of Christianity. There is nothing wrong with loving gaiety and parties. So, apparently, did Jesus, as we remember him at the wedding
feast at Cana (John 2:1-10). Not only do we assume that
he had a good time, but he wanted the guests to enjoy
themselves also. When the wine ran out, he turned the
water into wine and the festivities continued unabated.

But Christian joy goes far beyond pleasure, gaiety,
and happiness, although it may well include all three.
True joy is one side of the Christian coin; on the other is
suffering. Unless we share in the common suffering of

the world, which is also the suffering of our Lord, we cannot enter into his joy. The early Christians went to their deaths singing joyous hymns of praise. As it was their joy in the face of persecution and martyrdom that resulted in the conversion of many pagans two thousand years ago, so it is this same joy that effects conversions today. The unbeliever observes committed Christians and says, "I want what they have," and what they have, of course, is the Lord Jesus Christ.

"Rejoice in the Lord always: and again I say, Rejoice," Paul enjoins us (Phil. 4:4). These are words of healing, for in the joy of the Lord does indeed lie our strength (Neh. 8:10). It is this joy that undergirds all true worship, that leads us into heartfelt thanksgiving and ceaseless praise, that underlies our intercessions (for part of our joy is our knowledge that God hears and answers prayer). It underlies even our penitence, for there is inestimable joy in our certitude that God never fails to forgive.

The *fullness* of our joy, of course, can be found only within the kingdom of God, and Jesus said that in order to see the kingdom we must be born again. But, as Nicodemus asked, how can an adult person be born again? "No one can enter the kingdom of God without being born from water and spirit" (John 3:5).

Here our Lord enunciates the formula of Christian baptism as he proclaims the necessity of a spiritual regeneration "of water and of the Spirit." Thus many churches teach that in the sacrament of baptism we are born again, cleansed of sin, spiritually regenerated by the action of the Holy Spirit, and made members of the body of Christ.

None of the sacraments, including baptism, is magic,

however. If, as is the custom in many of the established churches, we are baptized as infants and live our entire adult lives apart from God and in sin, the fact that we were baptized will not save us, nor will the fact that as baptized Christians we may give lukewarm assent to whatever portions of the gospel we choose to believe, live by the Golden Rule, and attend church every Sunday. It is necessary, as our Lord made clear, that we be consciously aware of being born again, or more accurately, born from above of God.

What then is this rebirth experience? What actually happens, and how does it affect us?

For the purpose of simplification, rebirth can be equated with conversion. The two are not precisely the same, because the word *conversion* as we use it generally applies to someone who has never known Christ, while the new-birth experience applies most often to those who have known and believed in him, but less than completely. Nonetheless, conversion and rebirth have much in common.

When the experience of rebirth occurs suddenly and dramatically, there is an unforgettable moment of glorious truth, occasioned by the strong action of the Holy Spirit, when you accept entirely—not just with your mind, but with your heart and spirit and your whole being—the stupendous fact that Jesus is indeed your personal Savior and Redeemer. It is in this moment that you recognize the extent of your sins, experience the miracle of God's absolving grace, and commit your life utterly and without reservation to your Lord. The grace of the Holy Spirit, whom you received in baptism, is conveyed now in a new and fuller way.

When this new birth takes place, you, as a born-again Christian, know experientially the reality of God's love and the redemptive grace of Christ. You have appropriated the gift received in baptism. This experiential knowledge of your spirit given by the Holy Spirit may come in a variety of ways. Don't expect everyone's experience to be exactly like yours.

There are many for whom it is a gradual and scarcely perceptible awakening. These individuals cannot pinpoint in time the moment when they became aware of the reality of Jesus Christ and embraced not only his teachings but himself. As far as they can remember, they have always known and accepted with joy their relationship with God. It cannot be overemphasized that the born-again experience need not necessarily involve an instantaneous emotional reaction.

Each one of us experiences and is given to appropriate in a different way that new life in Christ that became ours at baptism. The important thing to realize is this: Even if our born-again experience comes to us as a great flash of lightning, even if we know the precise instant when we were made new in Christ, this experience is never a static thing. No Christian ever "has it made," for our "Yes" to Christ is a continuous and ongoing process that will never cease as long as we live.

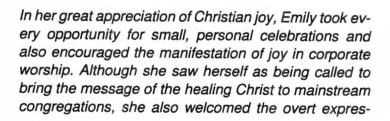

In her great appreciation of Christian joy, Emily took every opportunity for small, personal celebrations and also encouraged the manifestation of joy in corporate worship. Although she saw herself as being called to bring the message of the healing Christ to mainstream congregations, she also welcomed the overt expres-

sions of joy that occur so often in charismatic gatherings. She perceived upraised hands and vocal expressions of praise as conveying energy, excitement, and power and very often attesting the presence of the Spirit of God. Emily did see dangers, however, in some abuses, of which she speaks here. In the midst of the regrettable controversies and divisions that sometimes arise from overenthusiasm, she tried to stand always open to the power and action of the Spirit. And, typically, she tried to evaluate both the blessings of the gifts and their occasional abuses in an even-handed way.

Spiritually speaking, we are living today in wonderful, exciting, and curiously paradoxical times. On the one hand, many are predicting the demise of the institutional church, while on the other, we are witnessing extraordinary manifestations of the Holy Spirit that bring joy to the heart of every believer. Yet our joy is tempered by the knowledge that from time to time throughout the history of the church there have been comparable periods of holy fire that have flamed through Christendom, only to burn out because of our abuse of the gifts bestowed upon us by the Spirit of God. These same abuses and excesses are once again becoming all too evident. However, if we are fully aware of the dangers confronting us, there is no reason why the dismal history of the past need be repeated.

What is known as the charismatic movement has become, in many minds, erroneously synonymous with *glossolalia* (speaking in unknown tongues). Actually the charismata include all gifts of the Spirit (1 Cor. 12), of which many are being manifested today. Saint Paul makes clear that the Holy Spirit distributes different gifts to different people. In other words, all Christians do not necessarily have all or the same gifts. It is the *Holy Spirit*—the third person of the Trinity—who enables, empowers, and fills us with all joy, not the Holy Spirit's *gifts*. The gifts edify and strengthen the church, but they are not essential to her existence; only the Holy Spirit is indispensable.

For years we have neglected the work of the Holy Spirit. We didn't really know, or think about, just who the Holy Spirit is. The result is that today, with our new knowledge, many of us tend to overreact to the current charismatic emphasis on the Holy Spirit. For example, a man remarked to me not long ago, "Of course the Holy Spirit is *central.*" My reply was a quick "No." The Spirit is coequal and coeternal with the Father and the Son, God active in our lives. The Holy Spirit is the power of the Trinity and was active in our Lord's earthly life from beginning to end. Nevertheless, it is not the Holy Spirit but Jesus Christ who is central to our faith.

The term *neo-Pentecostal* is a misnomer. The true Pentecostal experience is not speaking in an unknown or nonexistent tongue; it is speaking in a foreign language intellectually unknown to the speaker. The Holy Spirit speaks through that person to others in their own language so that the word of God may be understood by the listener. On the day of Pentecost nearly two thousand years ago, those gathered together in one place "were all filled with the Holy Ghost, and began to speak with other tongues, as the Spirit gave them utterance—and the multitude were confounded, because that every man heard them speak in his own language" (Acts 2:4, 6).

On that day of the first Pentecost, Peter said, "Repent, and be baptized every one of you in the name of Jesus Christ for the remission of sins, and ye shall receive the gift of the Holy Ghost." Then Peter goes on to say, "For the promise is unto you, and to your children" (Acts 2:38-39), and this means us—you and me.

According to Scripture, then, when you are baptized, you receive the Holy Spirit, and thus it is erroneous to regard glossolalia as the sole sign of having received the Spirit of God. As I see so many around running from meeting to meeting frenetically striving to acquire tongues, I am torn between joy that so many want more of God and apprehension as to *why* they are seeking this particular gift rather than, let us say, the gift of wisdom. I think it behooves us all to check carefully our motives. Have we a sincere desire to strengthen the body of Christ, regardless of the cost to ourselves? Or could it be that we are seeking so frantically simply for our own self-gratification? Could it be, as I heard one man honestly state, our desire or what we think is our need to "blow off steam"? Could it be the weakness of our faith, which demands a "sign"? Could it be that we seek an emotional "kick" or wish to seem more "spiritual," more favored by God, than others? The answers to these questions will be given us in quiet prayer.

The gifts of the Spirit are for Christian service and vary in the faithful according to God's purpose for each individual; however, gifts and service are not in themselves evidence of spirituality. The church in Corinth had the gift of tongues, yet this church was carnal and corrupt, grossly misusing the gift. This is precisely why Saint Paul devoted so much space to the subject in his first epistle to the Corinthians.

Today the situation in many of our churches is much the same as at Corinth. Tongues too often have proved destructively divisive, splitting churches between the "haves" and the "have nots"; and many who speak in tongues are manipulative and spiritually arrogant. In such cases one must conclude that the phenomenon of glossolalia is not always of God. But we should never overlook those involved in the charismatic movement who are keenly aware of the abuses within the movement, who are amenable to suggestion and criticism, who are perpetually vigilant against spiritual pride and honestly strive to work within the framework of the church. To such as these, we all owe a debt of gratitude.

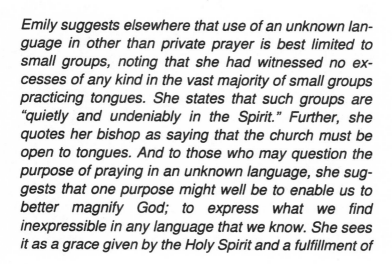

Emily suggests elsewhere that use of an unknown language in other than private prayer is best limited to small groups, noting that she had witnessed no excesses of any kind in the vast majority of small groups practicing tongues. She states that such groups are "quietly and undeniably in the Spirit." Further, she quotes her bishop as saying that the church must be open to tongues. And to those who may question the purpose of praying in an unknown language, she suggests that one purpose might well be to enable us to better magnify God; to express what we find inexpressible in any language that we know. She sees it as a grace given by the Holy Spirit and a fulfillment of

Jesus' promise: "And these signs shall follow them that believe; In my name . . . they shall speak with new tongues" (Mark 16:17). For her, this seems reason enough to seek and prize the gift.

Here, Emily considers some of the other charismatic gifts.

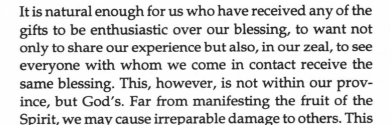

It is natural enough for us who have received any of the gifts to be enthusiastic over our blessing, to want not only to share our experience but also, in our zeal, to see everyone with whom we come in contact receive the same blessing. This, however, is not within our province, but God's. Far from manifesting the fruit of the Spirit, we may cause irreparable damage to others. This danger exists with *all* the gifts of the Spirit, all of which are subject to abuse.

There are those, for example, who claim the gift of healing and refuse to work under the authority of the church. I know too many such individuals who make the rounds of hospitals, unasked, and who, laying hands on a hapless patient, say, "Now you're healed. Go home." The results can be devastating.

Then there is exorcism, which is part of the healing picture. In my opinion, this is dangerous and should never be done lightly. If time and circumstances allow, it should be done under controlled conditions. Nor should it be done indiscriminately, but only if an individual requests it. Yet there are those who habitually tell anyone who is ill or disturbed that he or she is demon-possessed. They then proceed immediately, with no preparation, to exorcise the patient. If there is no response, the patient now has to struggle not only with illness but also with the idea of being possessed.

In many charismatic groups there seems to be an undue emphasis on Satan, an emphasis that culminates in the age-old heresy of dualism, where Satan and God are considered coequal adversaries.

Personally, I find it impossible not to believe in Satan. But to consider him equally powerful with God, who in Christ has won the victory, is inconsistent with the Christian faith. To refuse to acknowledge that Satan exists seems to me to fall into his trap. To make him the scapegoat for our personal sins is an easy way out of individual responsibility. To concentrate on Satan equally with, and sometimes to the virtual exclusion of, God is heresy.

I remember well my discomfiture when I found myself inadvertently participating in a small healing service with someone who seemed greatly overfocused on Satan. We both laid hands on each supplicant, alternating our prayers. Not once did my partner mention the name of God affirmatively: Each prayer dealt exclusively with casting out Satan.

The gift of prophecy likewise is subject to dangerous abuse. I know many with a genuine gift in the New Testament sense of delivering God's message to us today. Yet I know others who claim the gift of prophecy who are doing untold harm. These will say, for example, to one who is very ill, "The Lord told me that on April thirteenth at five in the afternoon, you will be healed." These self-termed prophets leave in their wake an anguished trail of unfulfillment. Not only should *no one* have the temerity to set dates and times of healing, but no one should *ever promise* a physical healing to anyone.

I have seen damage caused to many lives. I have seen emotional disturbances, mental derangements, and harm done the physically sick by abuse of the gifts. I have seen spiritual pride engendered in the cults that have begun outside the church. I have seen marriages destroyed because the partner of the one who has a gift has not the same gift. All these things are particularly heinous because they are done in the name of Jesus. During the past few years thousands have been blessed by one or more gifts of the Spirit, through which the church has been edified. However, if we fail to exercise due vigilance, I am fearful that what might have been a glorious outpouring of God's Spirit upon all flesh may end instead in ever more ungodly excesses.

If we follow as the Spirit of God leads us into all truth, we will never take our eyes from the Lord Jesus. If we strive to follow him, to align our wills with his, we can come to no harm, nor will we ever harm others.

Some Helpful Practices

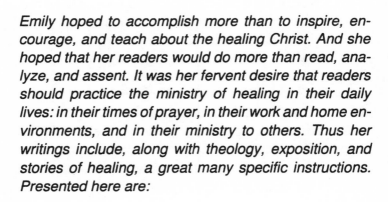

Emily hoped to accomplish more than to inspire, encourage, and teach about the healing Christ. And she hoped that her readers would do more than read, analyze, and assent. It was her fervent desire that readers should practice the ministry of healing in their daily lives: in their times of prayer, in their work and home environments, and in their ministry to others. Thus her writings include, along with theology, exposition, and stories of healing, a great many specific instructions. Presented here are:

- *a 30-day plan for strengthening faith*

- *an antidote to the poison of anxiety*

- *instructions on preparing a spiritual climate for healing (a handy summary of some essentials mentioned throughout this book)*

- *suggestions for ministering to others*

There are, of course, no formulas for healing, but Emily gives us many spiritual how-to's—signposts on the road to wholeness.

A thirty-day plan for strengthening faith

Some months ago a man came to me who had staggering problems, emotional, physical, and spiritual. He was quick to admit that he was only a lip-service Christian, but he had a truly sincere desire to know his Lord. To this man I submitted a plan that has proved extremely effective for countless individuals. I submit it here for you, for whether your faith is strong or weak, this is an exercise I believe all of us could undertake with benefit once or twice a year.

Surround yourself as much as possible with believers; try to affiliate yourself with a prayer group, and attend healing services regularly, for here you will find yourself in an atmosphere of almost palpable faith. Then undertake what I call the thirty-day experiment of faith. For a period of one month, act and live the promises of Jesus as if you believed with the fervency of the early Christians.

For thirty days, awaken each morning with the name of Jesus on your lips. Before getting out of bed, offer him praise and thanksgiving for another day, and offer your life for that day, praying that the Holy Spirit will guide you in all you do and say.

For thirty days, pray regularly, if only for a few minutes, morning, noon, and night, and throughout the day observe the presence of God by frequently offering brief sentence-prayers of praise.

For thirty days, read fifteen minutes a day of the New Testament, always asking first the guidance of the Holy Spirit. Read with special care of the Lord's healing miracles, as if you really believe that he is the same yesterday, today, and forever. Read all of the First Epistle of Saint John each week. This is a short epistle, and so filled with the love of God that no one who reads it under the guidance of the Spirit can fail to respond.

Before going to sleep at night, ask forgiveness of God for any sin you may have committed, and believe that you are forgiven. Finally, ask yourself whether you have done one thing that day because Christ said to do it, or whether that day you have abstained from one thing because he said *not* to do it. I suggest this final exercise for an important reason: It is a curious thing that while true faith leads to obedience, the converse is likewise true—obedience leads to a viable faith.

At the end of the month, if your desire to believe wholly in Christ has been strong and sincere, you are virtually assured of finding yourself with an undaunted faith and the courage to claim his promises in your own life. He will honor your faith, and your life will be transfigured.

An antidote to the poison of anxiety: Living in the present moment

I offer here two practical suggestions. First, if you are suffering from anxiety, share your apprehension with only one person—someone you can trust. To broadcast your worries far and wide only magnifies them.

Second, practice living in what the French theologian Jean-Pierre de Caussade calls "the sacrament of the present moment." This is a difficult concept, which will take time to put into effect, but keep trying, for it is well worth the effort.

In brief, the idea consists of abandoning yourself to the will of God, moment by moment. Do not worry about God's will either in retrospect or in advance; just try to live in the serenity of God's present intention for you. Center your attention on God's grace and will as they bear upon you instant by instant. Once you are centered in the present moment (neither in the past nor the future), this continuing act of surrender becomes a simple, joyous, and infinitely wonderful thing. It "works," as I know from personal experience. This does not mean that in your life there will never be trouble or anxiety or tension, but it does mean that these things will be caught up in the flood of God's love and mercy, moment by moment.

Anyone can learn to enter the present moment and surrender. Ask what God wants of you now (not tomorrow or next week). Ask the Holy Spirit to open your spiritual ears so that you may hear the response.

As you gradually learn to abandon yourself to God's

will and plan for you, instant by instant, your remorse over the past will lessen and your worry over the future will diminish. Unimpeded by either past or future, you will find yourself living in the fullness of life in the present, and you will experience in a new way the peace of God—or, more accurately, peace with God.

This is the peace that is not of this world. It is a peace that exists in your heart regardless of what has happened in the past or what may happen in the future. It is a peace that, regardless of trial and tribulation, lies at the core of our being and cannot be disturbed no matter what happens to us outwardly. It is the peace that can be found only in our certain knowledge that God lives, that he dwells in us and we in him. And so long as this is true, there is no room within us to harbor undue anxiety or fear.

Instructions on preparing a spiritual climate for healing

Although we may not know why everyone is not healed, we do know something of the conditions which, generally speaking, must be met if we are to be made whole. We know the necessity of establishing and living in a spiritual climate that will best enable us to receive God's healing power.

Searching out our sins: Asking the guidance of the Holy Spirit, we examine ourselves, seeking to find, to recognize, and to call by name those sins that separate us from God. We may not be guilty of any overt sins, but we may find ourselves surprised at the resentments, jealousies, envy, feelings of hostility, and similar sins of the spirit that we are harboring—all of which set up a barrier to the inflow of Christ's love in our lives.

Little by little those spiritual sins that may be separating us from God and hindering his healing power will be unearthed. The next step is to get rid of them, which is often far from easy.

Releasing our sins: I used to say glibly, "Just release these sins to God," but I have learned how difficult this can be. I submit here two techniques that, although they may appear childish, have helped many, including me.

Say, for example, you are dealing with jealousy. Write on a slip of paper the word "jealousy." Pray that God will forgive and remove it; ask God's blessing upon the individual against whom your destructive emotion is directed. Then burn the slip of paper and watch it burn. In this symbolic act there is an element of realism. You are relegating your sin to flame and nothingness. The remark of a woman uncontrollably jealous of a member of her prayer group is typical of many. "It sounds fantastic," she said, "but my jealousy disintegrated along with the paper. There's not a vestige left!"

Another effective technique is to write on a slip of paper both your sin and the name of the person against whom it is directed. Then place the slip in an unused Bible. In doing this, you are symbolically placing and leaving the situation with God.

Overcoming bitterness: A woman came to me who was filled with bitterness against the man to whom she had been married for twenty-five years. Their life together was filled with bickering and hostility. From the human point of view, the situation appeared hopeless. After praying each time we were together that Christ's love might overshadow this marriage and restore all brokenness, I told her that I would not see her again until she agreed to hold up her husband each day in the love of Christ, asking God to bless him, asking forgiveness for her inability to love (however justified this inability might seem), and praying that God would enable her to love.

About three months later she came to me and with wonderment in her voice said, "You know, I prayed as you told me for a long time. Then suddenly one day I realized I hadn't prayed that way for weeks. I realized that it wasn't because I had forgotten, but that it was no longer necessary. God had answered me, and I had come at last to love my husband."

Forgiving: If we are to receive God's healing grace, we must become open channels through which his power can flow—and lack of forgiveness on our parts clogs that channel with particles of resentment, or envy or hate or self-pity. These constitute the cholesterol of the soul. The dissolvent for this spiritual cholesterol is forgiveness.

The best way I know to help us forgive those who have trespassed against us is to think of what Christ has done for us. If we fail to accept in our hearts the fact that we are pardoned sinners, if we fail to live in the knowledge of God's merciful forgiveness, we ourselves cannot possibly forgive.

Once having learned to forgive, gotten rid of those factors that hinder God's healing power in our lives, the soil for healing is prepared. But there are still conditions to be met before the climate is established.

Giving thanks: An attitude of thanksgiving is an essential element of the healing climate. It is easy enough to be thankful when all goes well, but perhaps we cannot know the full meaning of thanksgiving until things have gone badly. In my own experience it has been within the context of pain that I have learned best how to be truly thankful.

For over two and a half years, for example, I was unable to sit upright with my legs outstretched. This meant that I could not take a hot bath, and anyone with a bad back knows the relief afforded by a tub of hot water. The first time I was able to lower myself into a bathtub still stands out in my memory as a momentous event, and I have never forgotten my inexpressible gratitude to God. Every single day since that memorable occasion, as I step into a hot bath I fervently thank God that I am able to do so. Such a small thing, but for me it was, and still is, a minor miracle!

No matter how bad things may be, we can always find something to be thankful for. The continual offering of our thanksgiving for things great and small becomes habitual with practice. When it becomes habitual, we have established an attitude indispensable to healing, whether of mind, body, or spirit.

Obeying: Obedience leads us to the kingdom, and obedience springs from love. It is out of the love we bear for Christ that we are constrained to obey. Whether or not we understand why Christ commands us to do certain things matters not at all. What does matter is that we do what he tells us to do.

Trusting: Finally, I would mention trust, which is the other side of the coin of faith and an intrinsic part of a total faith. For it is quite possible to have dynamic faith and still lack that quiet trust essential to the healing climate. To the precise extent that we trust God we are enabled to live in peace, without fear for today or apprehension for the future. Self-reliance is considered a highly commendable virtue in our culture, but unless we are willing to substitute God-dependence for self-reliance, we can never know the meaning of true security.

Suggestions for ministering to others

Those who know the healing Christ have a strong desire to take their knowledge and love out into the world, to minister for his sake to suffering friends and neighbors. Almost daily, laypeople query me as to how this may best be done. I address myself here to some questions frequently asked.

How should I approach the sick who may know nothing of, or do not believe in, the healing ministry?

The thing *not* to do is assault the sick with your knowledge that Christ heals. If you do this, you are likely to frighten them, for they may think you know something they have not been told; or you will so thoroughly antagonize them that you will never be able to convey your message.

When asked to visit such an individual by believing (or desperate) family members, I have found the best procedure is to go quietly into the sickroom, visiting casually and briefly. When it is almost time to leave, broach the subject by asking, "Do you know anything about the healing ministry?"

If the answer is no, remind them that more than one-third of the Gospels is devoted to our Lord's earthly healing ministry, and that it is recorded that he healed all who came to him. Remind the patient that Christ is the same yesterday, today, and forever; briefly describe the early post-apostolic church, in which healing was expected and received; explain today's revival of the church's ministry of healing; and mention some of the wonderful things that are happening as a result. If you feel an impulse to pray for the sick person, ask if you may do so. In the majority of cases, the patient is delighted. If members of the family are present, suggest that they (and the patient if able) might like to do some further reading concerning the healing ministry, and leave with them some pamphlets and a list of books. Suggest to the family that they attend healing services as intercessors.

If you find such patients alone when you visit, offer not only to hold them in prayer during the week but to attend healing services on their behalf, and ask them to be in prayer at approximately the same time.

If it happens that a patient does know anything about the healing ministry and states, "Yes—and I don't believe a word of it," this is your cue to strike a light note. In such cases I have found it helpful to say something like, "Well, I believe in it. I have to on the basis of Scripture and what I've seen happen in so many lives." Then I go on, "How about indulging me, even if you don't believe, and letting me say a prayer with you?"

I have had some amusing experiences with this approach. In one case, for example, a man whose wife had asked me to visit him watched television the entire time I was praying. Nonetheless, this man, who was critically ill, took a dramatic turn for the better two hours later. Healings under these conditions lead to the next question.

How important is the faith of the person who is ill?
While helpful, the patient's faith is not necessarily es-

sential. However, there must be faith somewhere. The man who watched television during the healing prayer may have had little or no faith, but I, who was ministering to him, believed. With the very sick we should not demand a miracle-working faith, for this takes an energy they do not possess. Rather we who believe should offer to exercise faith for them.

Should I lay hands on the sick?

This is a question which, in my opinion, cannot be answered by a categorical "Yes" or "No." The laying-on of hands, while itself not a sacrament, is a sacramental rite, and therefore should not be used indiscriminately by people who have no concept of what they are doing or why; nor should it be received by individuals without some explanation, lest the healing rite be misconstrued as magic. Incalculable harm has been done the healing ministry by those who have great zeal but no knowledge.

It is my belief that those who feel a vocation to lay on hands should do so always under the aegis of the church. In the healing ministry, one is handling the power of God, and this requires emotional balance—a balance that seems to be virtually impossible to maintain without the stabilizing influence of the church. In general, the safest rule to follow is simply to pray, holding the hand of the patient. If the one in need is a member of your own family, by all means lay on hands whether or not you feel you have a "vocation"; for love is the greatest healing force on earth.

What about ministering to someone who is unconscious?

Talk and act as if the person can hear every word you

say. Take the patient's hand if you can; explain briefly about the healing Christ, the will of God for wholeness, and God's power to mend all brokenness. Then offer aloud your prayer for healing.

There have been occasions when I have done this and a nurse has walked into the room, saying, "Don't you know this patient is in a coma and can't hear a word you say?" I just nod and go on praying, for there have been numerous times when a patient emerges from a coma days later and remembers every word and prayer that has been uttered. The ears may not hear at the time, but the spirit never sleeps and is never unconscious.

I recall vividly the case of a man desperately ill. The man knew his condition and remarked that he had never had an experience of God and was afraid to die. With these words, he lapsed into a coma.

I drew up a chair close to his bed and read to him portions of Scripture. Then I asked the unconscious man to picture our Lord at sundown at the end of a long day. Jesus was very tired, and when he came out from the house in which he was staying, he saw the streets lined with pallets on which lay the sick and dying. Our Lord forgot his fatigue, and in mercy and love he ministered to each and every one, and all were made whole (Luke 4: 40).

I spoke a few words about Jesus' love for the sick man lying in a coma, of how he knew exactly what was happening, and even then stood beside the bed, stretching out his hand to heal. Then I left the room.

The next morning the man's wife called me, her voice jubilant. Her husband had recovered consciousness and had asked to see me. That afternoon I found him sitting up in bed, his face radiant. His first words were, "I experienced the love of God last night. Never have I known such joy and peace." Then he went on to say, "How could anyone knowing this love ever be afraid to die? I know I'm not, anymore."

This man did not die; from that day on he made a swift recovery.

CHAPTER SEVEN

Living in Community
A Personal Journal

----◆----

In the mid-1970s Emily experienced "a strong premonition" of drastic change in her life. She had at one time felt a vocation to the religious life, but later came to believe that her work in leading missions and healing services, and in counseling, best expressed God's primary will for her. She did, however, continue to visit and came to know well a number of religious communities, both Roman Catholic and Anglican.

During a mission in Ohio she met Sister Virginia of the Episcopal Community of the Transfiguration. They became close friends, and Emily spent occasional weekends at the convent. Then one day she received a letter that was to signal the anticipated change in her life. Sister Virginia wrote her of an apartment on the convent grounds that would soon be vacant. After weeks of prayer, discussion with her bishop, and considerable anguish, she was led to a decision in prayerful awareness of the words, "The Lord, your God, is with you wherever you go" (Josh. 1:9).

Thus it came about that Emily moved to an apart-

ment—actually half of a small cottage—on the grounds of the Convent of the Transfiguration in Glendale, Ohio, a northern suburb of Cincinnati. Her commission there was to counsel the Sisters one day each week and to lead a monthly healing service. Feeling that she also must continue in parish work, doing what she had done at Calvary Church in Pittsburgh, she soon arranged to conduct weekly healing services at St. Thomas Episcopal Church in Terrace Park. It was the beginning of a new way of life, which Emily describes in her seventh and last book, The Healing Ministry: A Personal Journal.

In this book, Emily takes us through the church year, beginning with the feast of the Epiphany on January 6. Her observations on the Christian feasts and seasons bring out their relationships to the ministry of healing. She often remarked that the healing ministry illumines all other facets of the Christian faith, and in the same way her reflections on the church's great traditional observances shed new light on the wholeness and holiness that the healing ministry seeks.

Interwoven with this theme are accounts of her ongoing adventures in mission, her new "beloved friends" at St. Thomas Church, her deep friendships with the Sisters at the convent, and other delightful personal stories. In journal fashion, this book is episodic, the author reflecting on events as they occur. And as in any journal, some entries are brief some are detailed. Emily regarded this book, as did many of her readers, as embodying the spiritual fruits of her mature years.

◆

Settling In: The Early Months

January 6
The Epiphany of our Lord

Tonight is the monthly healing service in the convent chapel, and I still have the meditation to prepare. But it isn't difficult to speak about the healing Christ on Epiphany, which is the Church's feast day in commemoration of the coming of the magi, the first manifestation of our Lord to the Gentiles. I always think of the healing ministry as the "Epiphany ministry," for it is one of the means by which Jesus reveals himself, with stunning clarity, to the peoples of the earth. It uniquely shows forth the love and power of Jesus. It is the gospel in action.

Much as I love the chapel where Evensong and Sunday Mass are sung, I also love the modern oratory within the convent where daily Mass and the offices are said. Like most religious communities today, this one observes four of the monastic offices daily. Each one of these consists largely of portions of Psalms, which the church has always considered its most important book of prayer. The Psalms were the prayers of the prophets, the prayers of Jesus, and they seem to bring him very close.

The early morning office of Lauds is, to me, the most beautiful of all the hours. It is an hour of praise and preparation for the day that lies ahead. Following closely the church year, the climax of Lauds is invariably the Benedictus, the Song of Zechariah, that great hymn in praise of our redemption: "Blessed be the Lord God of Israel, for he has visited and redeemed his people."

Compline, the last prayer before sleep, is more subjective than the other offices. It is a prayer for the soul who makes her peace with God, a prayer for protection from the power of darkness, a prayer for all souls, everywhere.

Three times each day, morning, noon, and night, the Angelus is said in commemoration of the Incarnation of our Lord. "The angel of the Lord announced unto Mary, and she conceived by the Holy Spirit."

The chapel bell rings out each noon for the Angelus. It is good to have a reminder in the middle of the day, to stop briefly to pray.

My Lord, I love you and thank you for bringing me here.

January 25
Conversion of Saint Paul

Paul on the road to Damascus—the sudden flash of light—and he falls to the ground. Then the voice: "Saul, Saul, why do you persecute me?" Saul's question: "Who are you, Lord?"; and the answer: "I am Jesus, whom you are persecuting" (Acts 9:4-5).

I think of this on today's feast day, and of the times without number I have seen people brought to Christ through the healing ministry as they come face to face with the living God. Sometimes it is a Damascus road experience, but more often it is a slow, growing process through which the heart gradually opens so that one is able to receive more and more of what God stands ready and eager to give: himself. Then, as a bonus, if you will, we come to realize that "God will supply your needs fully, in a way worthy of his magnificent riches in Christ Jesus" (Phil. 4:19). One of my own greatest blessings has been the discovery that when we know Jesus, those things that used to seem all-important now fade into insignificance. Like Paul, we "come to rate all as loss in the light of the surpassing knowledge of my Lord Jesus Christ" (Phil. 3:8).

Looking out the window, I see a few snowflakes lazily drifting down, and my mind reverts again to the most recent mission. I remember the discussion time when someone stated, "I'm a Christian, I keep the Ten Commandments." So many are under the impression that this is all the Christian faith requires. Obviously the Ten Commandments must be kept, but the mere keeping of them does not make any one of us a Christian.

I remember, too, at this same mission, how someone asserted that the Golden Rule is Christianity in action. With this statement I have to quarrel. It's the same thing that pertains to the Ten Commandments: A good Christian must certainly follow the Golden Rule, but the mere following of it does not necessarily make one a good Christian.

Christianity is not mere intellectual assent or the observance of certain rules. It is the following of a certain person. The important thing is that we know the value of a personal experience of Christ, however it may come about, for without it we dare not call ourselves Christians, and upon it depends our wholeness, our very life.

Someone whom I am counseling regularly but infrequently, as he lives far from Cincinnati, said to me last time I saw him, "All my life I've been a nominal Christian. I want to know Jesus, but I'm discouraged. I don't even know what it is to 'experience' Christ." This is nothing to be ashamed of. The real danger lies in not acknowledging this truth to ourselves.

There are a number of things that those who are hungry to experience Christ may do. The first thing is to acknowledge, as did this man, that we do not know him, even though we may know all about him. A genuine surrender on our parts is a necessity if we would experience Christ, and this is not easy. There must be a determination to die daily to self, to decrease so that he may increase, to be willing to give all for his sake: Those material things to which we are inordinately attached, our associations, desires, ideas, ambitions, our doubts and fears and sins. It is in our giving of all these things that, in essence, constitute ourselves that Christ makes himself known to us, in different ways to different people.

Our quest for the knowledge and love of God; our desire to obey unfalteringly, for we inevitably falter; our gradually increasing sensitivity to the leading of the Spirit—all these comprise an ongoing, never-ending process. Love, faith, obedience, self-abandonment to God—these are the flagstones that pave the way to the kingdom. It is neither a smooth nor an easy road to traverse. Jesus never said it would be. But it is the most exciting and wonderful road in the world.

The healing ministry has to a great extent recaptured the dynamism and the passion of the faith. However, this ministry, as is true of every aspect of the faith, is a costly thing. The rewards are beyond description and without price. Nevertheless, the cost cannot be denied. That is why this ministry will never become a truly "popular" ministry within the church. For this we can probably rejoice as we remember how Christianity became a nominal, largely lip-service religion when popularized by Constantine.

Where does the cost lie? It lies in involvement. All of us associated with the healing ministry in any way become deeply involved with those who suffer, and not with them only but with a suffering world.

It lies in obedience. To obey in order to receive God's blessings is a hopeless proposition. We can never be close to God unless we obey simply because we love. How can we love God more? Never by ourselves, but as Saint Paul tells us, by the Holy Spirit: "the love of God poured out in our hearts through the Holy Spirit who has been given to us" (Rom. 5:5).

Above, beyond, and undergirding all else, the cost is love: loving God, loving one another, loving the unlovable, and in so doing, becoming ourselves vulnerable. The only way we can be sure whether or not we love someone is to ask ourselves whether we are willing to pay the price of love. It is high. It can be the Cross.

Are we willing to pay it? Yes, because as Christians we know that by the Cross comes Resurrection.

February 2
Presentation of Christ

I awoke shivering. Turning up the electric blanket, I snuggled deeply into its warmth and switched on the weather radio just in time in hear: "The temperature at 4:00 A.M. was minus twenty-five degrees." At this news

I was strongly tempted to remain in my warm bed, say my prayers, and skip going out in the pitch-black, frigid cold to Mass.

I thought of the verse in one of the psalms we say daily at Lauds: "Let the saints be joyful with glory: let them rejoice in their beds" (Ps. 149:5). This morning I felt like rejoicing in my bed! But again, as always when similarly tempted, there flashed through my mind the parable of the banquet, and the feeble excuses of those invited as to why they could not attend (Luke 14:16-20). And besides, this is an important holy day. Mary and Joseph, obedient in all things, present Jesus in the temple following the law of Moses: "Every first-born male shall be consecrated to the Lord" (Luke 2:23). So, of course, I went, bundled up with two sweaters under my fur coat and a wool scarf over my face, leaving only my eyes uncovered. "O ye frost and cold, bless ye the Lord; O ye ice and snow, bless ye the Lord; praise him and magnify him forever."

The Healing of Memories

There is great emphasis today on inner healing: the healing of the memories. This is not a new method of prayer; Agnes Sanford wrote of it many years ago. However, the fact that it is being emphasized today has resulted perhaps in an increased sense of expectancy. Hence there are more such healings than ever before and often dramatic ones. This type of prayer consists of asking Jesus to go back in time in the life of the disturbed person, requesting that he heal the trauma of each phase of his or her life. Some degree of pastoral counseling (and frequently some psychotherapy) is ordinarily a concomitant to the prayer for inner healing. However, over the past several years I have noted a significant number of either instantaneous or very rapid healings when neither I nor anyone else has had any prior knowledge of the person involved. In addition to the usual advisability of counseling as an adjunct, the prayer for inner healing is so long as generally not to be possible at a public healing service. However, on more than one occasion, a person has traveled a great distance for one service and this specific prayer, and is unable to return.

I recall, for example, one woman who came up to the altar rail in a very agitated state and asked prayer for the healing of memories. I had never seen her before, and I explained that this prayer was too lengthy to pray under the circumstances. However, when she told me tearfully that she had flown into Cincinnati that day expressly to attend the service, and was flying home at midnight, I asked her to wait until the others had been ministered to, and then I would take her alone. This we did, I praying that the Holy Spirit would pray in me, making intercession according to the will of God, as I did not know how to pray (Rom. 8:26-27).

At the end of the prayer, she arose from her knees, radiant, her countenance replete with the peace of God that does indeed pass all understanding. I knew she had been healed, and together we thanked God.

She was extremely grateful to me, although obviously I had had nothing to do with the matter. As she left the church, she asked what she could do for me to express her gratitude. My request was twofold: first, I asked her to let me hear from her. She readily agreed and for two years has written regularly. Now that she had told me her full story, her instantaneous healing seems specially remarkable. She has also commented that the prayer led by the Spirit touched on those very areas of trauma in need of healing. (This did not seem in the least remarkable to me!) My second request was that every night before she went to sleep, she would pray, "Into your hands, Lord, I commend my spirit, and ask you to heal, while I sleep, everything within me that has need of healing." This, too, she has continued to do. It is an ideal way, incidentally, for any of us to drop off to sleep. I pray this prayer regularly for myself.

Most physicians concur that the fetus can be influenced by the attitude of the mother carrying the baby. Time and again I have had the validity of this theory confirmed in my own experience, which is why, when praying for the healing of memories, I go back not only to the person's childhood but to the time when the individual was *in utero*.

The importance of this first became apparent to me when, within a fairly brief period of time, a number of adoptive parents, experiencing trouble with their adopted children, came to me for counseling. Typical of these were a husband and wife, both committed Christians, both gentle and loving people, who had adopted a six-month-old baby girl ten years before. From the beginning, the infant was remarkably undemonstrative, refusing to be held and cuddled. Even when very small, she seemed filled with hostility and anger, rejecting all signs of affection by her adoptive parents. At the age of seven, she began to exhibit real cruelty, trying with deliberate calculation to hurt her parents. She was going on eleven when they sought me out.

As they talked, it suddenly became clear to me what the trouble probably was and that most of it must have occurred when the child was *in utero*. The couple sitting with me that day knew little of their child's natural mother, but what they knew (and what pertains in so many such cases) shed a great deal of light. The natural mother had become pregnant when she was a freshman in college. She was forced to leave college for a year, and that particular college, the one of her choice, refused to reinstate her. One can well imagine the anger and resentment the girl felt, which destructive emotions were visited upon the fetus.

After several sessions with the adoptive parents, I explained to them what the prayer for the healing of the memories was, and asked them to explain to the child as much as she was capable of comprehending. I then asked them to bring the little girl to me if they could do so without forcing her against her will.

Two weeks later they brought her. She was an attractive, albeit sullen, child. It became quickly evident that her emotional problems included deep feelings of rejection due to the fact that her natural mother had "given her away," as she put it. I explained to her that in the very beginning her mother was undoubtedly resentful and frightened, not knowing which way to turn. But I pointed out that she "loved you very much. She chose to have you, to give you life. When you were born she had to give you up because she loved you so much she wanted people to have you who could take very good care of you, as she could not."

I prayed that Jesus would go back in time to when this child was an embryo, asking that he touch that unborn baby and grant her the assurance that he loved her with an everlasting love. I prayed that he would give this baby the assurance that he had planned and wanted her to be born, and had known her name since the beginning of time. I prayed that he would grant her the certainty of mind that he had already chosen her adoptive parents, who would love her in his love. Then I asked Jesus to go to this child when she was an infant, taking her in his arms, saying, "I love you as much as though you were the only child in the entire world. Next to me, your father and mother love you. So accept this love, my child. It will be yours forever, no matter what you do."

At each stage of this little girl's life, including the present, I prayed that he would assure her of his unbounded love as well as the love of her parents in whose care he has placed her. I prayed that Jesus would heal now all the hurts of this child and enable her to accept his love and that of her parents.

When the prayer was concluded, tears were streaming down the girl's face, and she said, "Please, would you pray just one more thing?" When I said, "Of course, what?" she replied, "Please ask Jesus to forgive me for being so mean to Mommy and Daddy."

The love of God filled that room, and I knew that in her as in so many others a marvelous healing had taken place. From that day on, she manifested to her parents a new gentleness and an increasing receptivity to their love.

This sort of healing is not restricted to adopted children. Many adults have suffered the emotional consequences of being unwanted by their married parents. In most cases, after they were born, they were much loved and had happy childhoods. However, damage had been done while they were in the fetal stage, which had to be healed before they, as adults, could be whole.

Two questions recur pertaining to prayer for the healing of memories. The first: "Can I pray this prayer for myself?" The answer is "Yes," but in my experience this must be qualified by the comment that it seems more effective when prayed by someone else.

The second question is "Can I, as an intercessor, pray this prayer for someone else?"

For a long while I honestly did not know the answer. Only recently have I noted that in three successive cases this has been successfully done. In two of these three cases, the prayer was offered without the knowledge of the one prayed for. Generally speaking, however, it appears to be more effective to pray directly with the person concerned, and regardless of the reason for intercession, it is helpful if the person knows he or she is being prayed for and when.

Solemnities and Feasts

Ash Wednesday

Today is the first day of Lent and we received the imposition of ashes. Since the ninth century this rite has symbolized the penitence of the people of God.

The first time I heard the term "celebrating" Lent, it seemed to me incongruous to "celebrate" that season set apart by the church for penance. However, as I reflected upon it, it came to make good sense. *Lent* is an old English word meaning "spring," and spring is a time of growth and increase. This is certainly cause for celebration, as is the fact that although Lent and Holy Week take us through the Crucifixion, each passing day also brings us closer to the incredibly wonderful event upon which the faith is founded: the Resurrection.

I have just finished a good mission with many healings, but curiously, what remains most vividly in my mind are the morning discussion periods. These were dominated by a theme initiated by a young married woman in a wheelchair, incapacitated by multiple sclerosis. It was she who asked the first question: "If I am not healed, how can I possibly glorify God? I can't take care of my family. I can't do anything but sit in a wheelchair." This same question was immediately echoed by others who for one reason or another, whether because of age, illness, or young children whom they could not leave, felt they were not able to serve God as actively as they felt they should.

If I were granted one wish in regard to my work in the healing ministry, it would be that I might convey the certainty I feel that no matter what our condition, we are all within God's providence and that he is always in charge. The important thing is to *be* and not to *do*. The only time God cannot use us is if we make ourselves unavailable. Physical handicaps, illness, family circumstances give none of us the right to say "no" to God.

I know, beyond the shadow of a doubt, that whether we are flat on our backs awaiting healing or in perfect health, God will enable us to serve, perhaps to pray for those in need, perhaps to lend a sympathetic ear to those who need to talk, perhaps to attend healing services regularly to pray for and bolster the faith of others. I have learned both in my own life and by observation that God's promise to Paul is also a promise to us, namely, that God's grace is always sufficient.

We believe that God will make us whole, but while

we wait, there is important work for us to do. I asked the young woman in the wheelchair to invite God to work in her, assuring her that if she did, there would be a great change in her life, that others would notice this change, and she would be an inspiration to all who came in contact with her.

I remember a man recovering from deep depression who asked, "How could I possibly help anyone?" Anyone who has suffered from clinical depression can be of inestimable assistance to others who are enduring the same suffering, a suffering no one who has not undergone it can fully understand. I cannot understand it, but having seen so much of the agony it causes, I feel great compassion for its victims. However, I daresay those who have actually been through it could be more helpful to others in the same situation than can I.

Somewhere I read that more healings occur in Lent than at any other time of the year. This is not surprising, for the spiritual exercises suggested for Lent are precisely those we emphasize for the establishment of a climate for healing. If we are not already living by rule, Lent is a good time to start, using the Lenten discipline as a firm foundation. Most Christians are familiar with everything contained in the Lenten "invitation," with the possible exception of fasting. Fasting is of such importance that I continually wonder why so little attention is paid to it. The biblical concept of fasting is to abstain from food. If one's physical condition does not permit this, there are other ways to abstain. I suggest always that those who attend healing services come fasting as they are able. For working people, going all day without food may not be practical. In such cases I suggest a very light luncheon, and nothing more to eat until after the service. The ideal fast is, in my opinion, of twenty-four hours duration.

Remember always that fasting is a spiritual exercise to be done with our eyes on God. We do not fast as a means of bargaining or of winning God's approval. We fast out of love, as a way to give God glory.

Using the Ash Wednesday exhortation as the basis for a rule, I would add spiritual reading in addition to the Bible. Whatever material has been selected should be read slowly and reflectively. I suggested to "my" people at Saint Thomas on Monday night that during Lent they might wish to increase every aspect of their rule by five minutes each day: five minutes more of prayer, of Scripture reading, of spiritual reading.

March 12
Gregory the Great

I have a special feeling for Saint Gregory. I often urge those who are suffering in any way, including pain from such things as anxiety or frustration, to offer their brokenness to be used for God's glory and on behalf of someone they know who is in need of prayer. I suggest that they pray in their own words to this effect, "Lord, I offer to you my brokenness, praying that you will convert this to your holy purpose and use it for your glory. I pray also that you will use it on behalf of Mary or John, whose need is so great." I have found this to be an extremely powerful method of intercession, which at the same time transforms the suffering of the intercessor into a creative and redemptive thing.

I had long thought this way of prayer was my own discovery, based on Colossians 1:24. Then I learned that Saint Gregory had used this means of intercession nearly fourteen hundred years before my time! Every time I think I have made a new discovery in the spiritual life, invariably I find that someone else "discovered" it more than a thousand years ago. Recently I was cheered to read a comment by a well-known theologian: "If you think you have come up with a totally new idea, watch out: you are probably in heresy!"

In regard to "new ideas," I seem also to share a difficulty expressed by Thomas Merton: "You find out that your latest discovery is something you already found out five years ago." Nevertheless it is profoundly true, as Merton says, "that one penetrates deeper and deeper into the same ideas and the same experiences." In any event, much as I would love to study Scripture under St. Jerome, so I would love to learn more of prayer from Gregory the Great!

In view of the type of prayer I have been thinking about, and considering the kind of winter we are having here, it is not surprising that my mind flies back to the last winter I was at Calvary Church in Pittsburgh. One February night I was told that two busloads of people were coming from out of town to the healing service, and I had agreed to speak with them after the service. It was an exceptionally long service, and by the time I was finished and was ready to start home, it was after 11:30.

On that bitterly cold night, the roads were thickly glazed with ice. I was extremely tired, having been on my feet for hours, and my back was hurting badly. About halfway home, and after three unsuccessful tries at getting my car up what appeared to be a snow bank, I began to offer my fatigue and aching back to God to use on behalf of one of "my" people who was crippled by a bad back after two unsuccessful operations. The poor man had not been at the service that night, and I knew there must be a good reason for his absence. By the time I reached home well after midnight, all fatigue was forgotten, as was my own aching back.

The person for whom I had offered my problems in union with Christ was at Calvary the following Monday night. After the service he said, "The strangest thing happened last Monday night. I couldn't come to the service, I was simply too much in pain. About midnight, I suddenly had the sensation of being in a tub of hot water. The pain in my back just seeped out. I could feel it leaving. I went to sleep and woke up the next day without a vestige of pain, and I've had none since." Coincidence? No. Not when this sort of thing happens again and again.

Sister Virginia, always so strong and robust, is not looking well and seems strangely lacking in energy. We sit on opposite sides of the oratory, but I can always hear her clear voice above the others during Lauds. This morning even her voice sounded weak. I am concerned about her.

March 25
The Annunciation
Walking home from Mass this morning, I marveled at how, overnight, everything seems to have sprung to

life. Snow two days ago—and suddenly it's spring. The convent grounds are bright with the shining gold of forsythia and daffodils, and the magnolias are about to burst into bloom. Everything this month seems to emphasize death and resurrection.

I love this feast day because I love Mary, mother of our Lord: Mary, Star of the Sea. (For anyone who loves the sea as I do, I smile at God's determination to keep me from it. Brought up in New York in an era when anything west of Fifth Avenue was beyond the pale, I thought Pittsburgh, when we first moved there, was no man's land. Now it seems the "East," as I find myself in Cincinnati, indisputedly the Middle West.)

Mary is the perfect example of human obedience to God. I think of that young Jewish girl two thousand years ago, and how frightened she must have been at the awesome responsibility given her, to carry in her womb Jesus, the son of God. I think of her unhesitating response to the angel Gabriel, "Behold, I am the handmaid of the Lord; let it be to me according to your word" (Luke 1:38). Mary, the one whose supreme act of acquiescence to God's will, changed the world for all people and for all time.

Devotion to (not worship of) Mary as the mother of our Redeemer is almost as old as the church herself. Pictures drawn on the walls of the catacombs attest to this, while the belief in the efficacy of her intercessions is extremely ancient.

One difficulty for many Protestants, which I recognize and respect, is the fact that they do not believe that the saints, both living and dead, pray for us. This being so, they obviously cannot accept Mary as preeminent among the heavenly intercessors: Preeminent because of her sanctity and thus the power of her prayers; the closest to her son and therefore sharing a special place beside him; the queen of heaven, above angels and archangels and all the saints. However, rejection of Mary as intercessor does not preclude honoring her as the mother of God.

"The Mother of God?" someone said to me. "That is ridiculous!" But it is not. "Who was she the mother of?" I countered. "Why, Jesus, of course," came the reply. Precisely. And Jesus was truly God as well as truly man. Notwithstanding, many non-Roman Catholics seem to feel more comfortable with the term *Theotokos,* God-bearer, used by the eastern churches.

I readily admit that for a long time after I became a Christian, I had difficulty knowing what to "do" with Mary. I wanted no one, not even his mother, to come between me and Jesus. I was to learn much from a seventeen-year-old girl, not a Roman Catholic, who was dying of leukemia. The closer to death she came, the closer her relationship with the holy mother. I pondered this for a long time and finally came to understand.

Whatever we may or may not believe about the mother of our Lord, it is essential, as Christians, that we believe in the virgin birth.

"I can't see that it matters one way or the other," a young clergyman said to me not long ago. It matters very much indeed. How would the Incarnation have come about otherwise? How could Jesus have been fully God, if not conceived by the Holy Spirit? How fully man, if not born of woman? What would have happened to our salvation had Mary said to the messenger of the Lord, "No, thank you. I don't care to bear in my womb the Son of God conceived by the Holy Spirit?"

But the answer of this young girl to what must have been a terrifying proposal was an unreserved "Yes." "Let it be to me according to your word." This is a perfect healing prayer, denoting complete acquiescence to God's will and the acknowledgment that, according to the written Word, it is for our wholeness, however this is to come about.

Holy Week
Maundy Thursday

Today the Holy Triduum has begun, those last three days before Easter when we not only remember the Passion but participate as best we can in the suffering and death of Christ. It is evening and I have just returned from Mass. I feel chilly though the house is warm, so I make a cup of hot coffee. I reflect upon the service tonight, which seems to me in a very real sense to be our Lord's last will and testament. All that he has taught for the three years of his earthly ministry, he has summarized at the Last Supper.

The institution of the sacrament of his body and blood: "Mercifully grant that we may receive it thankfully in remembrance of Jesus Christ our Lord, who in these holy mysteries gives us a pledge of eternal life" (*Book of Common Prayer*).

The washing of his disciples' feet: "Do you understand what I just did for you? . . . What I just did was to give you an example: As I have done, so you must do" (John 13:12-15). For, Jesus said, "This is my commandment: love one another, as I have loved you" (John 15:12).

And, finally: "Peace is my farewell to you, my peace is my gift to you" (John 14:27). This is his gift of salvation.

After the Communion, a portion of the consecrated bread and wine is carried to the altar of repose, which is in the tiny side chapel of Saint Francis. The altar is stripped, the sanctuary light extinguished, and the church left in total darkness. The Light of the World has been put out, and people just like me have done it. Christ have mercy.

It is time now to return to the little chapel to keep my hour of the vigil. There is room for only three at a time, one on each side of the chapel, and one kneeling in the center before the altar. The two Sisters and I who have this hour together, silently meet, and wait to replace those who are concluding their hour of prayer. At midnight the reserved sacrament is placed in the tabernacle, and the chapel vigil is terminated.

Good Friday

The sound of trains in the night, usually pleasantly nostalgic, seemed unbearably sad last night.

Today we have the Mass of the Presanctified, celebrated since the seventh century. Immediately preceding this is the veneration of the cross. "This is the wood of the cross on which hung the Savior of the world," intones the priest. "Come let us worship," we respond. The cross is then placed at the entrance to the sanctuary, where the priest venerates it. Any desirous of doing so, walk quietly up and kneel.

The Reproaches are begun: "O my people, what have I done to thee? Or wherein have I wearied thee? Answer me."

"Holy God, Holy and Mighty, Holy and Immortal, have mercy upon us."

"We venerate thy Cross, O Lord, and we praise and glorify thy Holy Resurrection; for lo! by the Cross, joy hath come to the whole world."

The Sisters sing even more beautifully this year. It is moving to me that they rehearse so long and hard, only that they may sing well for the glory of God. For although anyone is welcome, the community encourages people to attend their own parish churches. Thus an outside congregation is virtually nonexistent.

On Ash Wednesday I spoke of "celebrating" Lent. But I find it impossible to celebrate today as I walk the road to Calvary with Jesus. "A great crowd of people followed him, including women who beat their breasts and lamented over him" (Luke 23:27). I am among these, and I hear Jesus say, "Daughters of Jerusalem, do not weep for me, but weep for yourselves and for your children" (Luke 23:28).

I see my Lord on his grim march to the scaffold, exhausted, staggering under the weight of the cross. I see him fall into the dust, then painfully rise again to continue his torturous way to be crucified between two thieves. And yet, bent now though he is, weary, begrimed, I never see a defeated man but only the King of Glory.

I come home from the chapel at three o'clock and wander around, aimlessly. I know with my mind that Easter will be here day after tomorrow, but emotionally I am totally depressed. From now until Easter are the most terrible—and the longest—hours of the entire year. I try to pray and cannot. I feel like one of the apostles, confused, bewildered, for my Lord has been crucified. I have the entirely irrational feeling that God is dead. But in my heart I am grateful for this feeling, however irrational I know it to be.

Living these long hours between the Crucifixion and the Resurrection, I am reminded of what life would be without God.

I think of the Roman centurion standing at the foot of the cross at Calvary, of how his spiritual eyes were gradually opened, so that when it was all over, he would blurt out, "Clearly this was the Son of God!" (Matt. 27:54). Each Good Friday that passes, my spiritual eyes, like those of the centurion, seem to open a little wider.

Holy Saturday

Today in the mail, I found a letter from Father Paul, a dear priest friend, who is joyfully awaiting his death. Father Paul has granted me the inestimable privilege of sharing in his dying. As I read his letter I realized how closely his words approximated the findings of Dr. Elisabeth Kubler-Ross, well-known for her research in the field of death and dying, as well as other psychiatrists who have joined her in this work. Their general conclusion is that there is definitely life after death. Their evidence is based on the reports of those who have gone through the death process and been resuscitated. Of course the Christian received his "proof" nearly two thousand years ago!

Pondering Father Paul's letter, my mind flew back to a religious conference of several years ago where I was the speaker. It was an annual one-day conference and very tightly scheduled. I was sitting in the sacristy, grateful to be alone for a few minutes before the evening healing service began. An Episcopal priest walked in, apologized for intruding, and then introduced himself. I looked into his eyes and involuntarily gasped. Then I heard myself say, "You have been with Jesus, haven't you?"

He nodded and said, "I don't know whether you have ever seen anyone who has been raised from the dead." Before I could say anything, the man went on, "You're looking at one now." This, then, explained the look in his eyes.

"I was raised from the dead fifteen years ago," he said, "I had crossed over and my death certificate had already been made out. I was filled with a joy so great I can't even begin to put it into words. Then I heard the most indescribably beautiful voice that said: 'You must go back. Your family needs you desperately.'"

Much as he loved his family, he was completely heartbroken that he could not remain with Jesus. Those moments of so-called death were so wonderful that it took him years to reconcile himself to the fact that he had been sent back here, that the conflict within himself after he returned and had to resume life was a battle he thought would never end. After, long, long months of prayer, he finally entered the ministry, where he is now deeply involved in healing.

"I have peace now," he said, "but I can hardly wait until I go again to stay with our blessed Lord."

Easter Sunday

In the darkness the fire is kindled in the back of the chapel, and the voice of the priest breaks into the stillness: "O God, through your Son you have bestowed upon your people the brightness of your light: Sanctify this new fire, and grant that in this paschal feast we may so burn with heavenly desires, that with pure minds we may attain to the festival of everlasting light" *(Book of Common Prayer)*.

The candle, now lighted, is borne down the center aisle. Three stops are made, at each one is sung, "The light of Christ," while we respond, "Thanks be to God." The small candles carried by the Sisters and each member of the congregation are lit from the paschal candle, which is then placed in its stand in the sanctuary.

By its light the Exsultet is sung, that paschal proclamation that, Thomas Merton declared, teaches all theology. And it does, for we are an Easter people living by the power of the risen Christ.

"Rejoice now, heavenly host and choirs of angels, and let your trumpets shout salvation for the victory of our mighty King."

Finally the candles on the altar are lit and it comes alive in a burst of dazzling brilliance. As the Eucharist is about to begin, I hear in my heart the exultant words, "Christ being raised from the dead will never die again; death no longer has dominion over him. . . . Since by a man came death, by a man has come also the resurrection of the dead. . . . For as in Adam all die, so also in Christ shall all be made alive."

Alleluia, Christ is risen. The Lord is risen indeed. Alleluia! And because he has, we need no longer fear death and thus can fully live.

Abundant Healings: Body, Mind, and Spirit

April 29
Catherine of Siena
I got very little sleep last night, but it was not a total

loss, as I practiced what I preach. First, I offered my sleeplessness to God, then prayed for every person and every cause I could think of: all who suffer in any way, all who are alone, all who lie sleepless in hospital beds, all physicians and nurses, the church, her clergy and people, the nation, the world.

Then I thought of Saint Catherine of Siena, whose feast day we celebrate today. She had great healing gifts that she used to the full as she worked, as a Dominican Tertiary, among the sick, particularly among lepers and cancer patients.

It is interesting to note that while many church people today tend to recoil from such phrases as "pleading the blood," Catherine begins a number of her letters, "I write to you in his precious blood," and then she bids those to whom she writes to "bathe" or "drown" themselves in the blood of Jesus. In her prayers for others, she frequently speaks of placing them in his blood. Perhaps it was her teaching which led me to pray as I do for certain people, notably leukemia patients, pleading for a mystical exchange of blood; praying that Christ's blood, whole, perfect, cleansing, redeeming, may flow through their bodies. As I look back and remember her well-known "Dialogue," I may well have had this in my unconscious mind when I began to emphasize the necessity of daily Communion for leukemia victims, regardless of their church affiliation. I can only believe that as a result, many medically incurable cases have been marvelously healed, or in remission for so long that they may be legitimately claimed as "healings."

As women today strive for a place in the sun, I smile to myself at the enormous influence exerted in the church by a young woman like Catherine, who lived in the fourteenth century. She worked tirelessly for the unity of the church, going to see Pope Gregory XI and prevailing upon him to return to Rome. Upon his death, when the great papal schism erupted, she deluged cardinals and monarchs with letters, urging them to support Urban VI. She was certainly a great deal more successful in influencing her church than any one of us who lives today!

Late this morning, Sister Virginia stopped by to tell me she had discovered a lump in her breast and would be entering the hospital in three days. Alas, I shall be far away on mission. We had prayer with the laying-on of hands, and I anointed her.

Rushing to do some errands, I stepped in a pothole and went sprawling, falling with my full weight on my right hand. By evening the hand was so badly swollen and discolored that I called one of the Sisters, who is a nurse, to look at it. "Sorry, Emily," she said, "I'm afraid it is broken."

She drove me at once to the emergency room of the nearest hospital, where we spent the next four hours. Saturday night is not the time to go to an emergency room.

Close to midnight, X-rays were at last taken. Shortly thereafter, a doctor came out and said that the hand was fractured, and a small piece of bone had been broken off. He then announced he would put the hand in a cast. I panicked at this news. I had the Methodist church healing service the next night, and was leaving on mission the day after. The healing power goes through my right hand, and in a cast how could I lay on hands? Sister realized the predicament and said she would speak to the doctor and see that the hand was not put in a cast if I insisted on keeping my engagements, which she, as a nurse, advised me not to do. I assured her I had led missions with far worse things than a broken hand.

I still have no idea what she told the doctor, but he came out scowling and said, "All right, if you insist, I'll put you in a splint instead." This he proceeded to do, with obvious disapproval.

All the way home from the hospital, Sister tried to dissuade me from doing the work next day. Obviously I could not cancel out at this late date, and she, God bless her, came over next morning at six-thirty to help me dress and put on make-up.

The people at the Methodist church were somewhat startled to see my hand, but the day went well, although the hand was very painful. There was a large crowd for the healing service, and precisely when it happened, I don't know. Suddenly, in the middle of the service when I was laying hands on someone, I became aware that my hand no longer hurt. I thanked God and continued. When I looked at my fingers later that evening, all swelling had gone, and there remained no sign of discoloration.

The mission on the following day was good, though I had trouble keeping my heart in and my mind on it because of my underlying concern for Sister Virginia. My first day there the convent had called me to say that she had just undergone a mastectomy. I wired her flowers and then, with something of a struggle, proceeded to the task at hand.

One of the most moving episodes of the mission concerned Bill, a former Roman Catholic priest who had left the ministry two years before to marry. As is so frequently the case under such circumstances, Bill was suffering all sorts of emotional upsets due to his inner conflict. He had urgently asked to see me during the mission, so we met one morning alone in the chapel.

He was depressed and withdrawn, one of his chief problems being a crisis of faith and the subsequent loss of any prayer life. After an hour of talk, he asked for prayer and the laying-on of hands. During the prayer there occurred that supernatural outpouring of God's love that for me signifies the actual presence of Jesus in our lives. Bill remained kneeling at the altar rail, while I knelt in a front pew. After perhaps ten minutes, he arose and came towards me with outstretched arms, his countenance transfigured with joy as tears streamed down his cheeks. This man, a few minutes before so depressed and withdrawn, now threw his arms around me and kept exclaiming, "He lives and I *know* it now. He lives and I know it!" I said to him, "No more doubts?" and he replied, "No, how could there be? He's *here*, I can *touch* him! I'll never forget this experience as long as I live." He was correct; once having tasted God one never completely forgets, though there may well come times when the memory dims. Then the embers of recollection must be rekindled and fanned into flame by the breath of the Holy Spirit and our own desire.

A Sister met me at the airport so that we could stop by

the hospital to see Sister Virginia before coming home to the convent. I was appalled at how Sister Virginia looked, and hoped my shock was not apparent.

We prayed and I anointed her. (Given permission by my bishop to anoint, I always carry blessed oil in my purse.) As we embraced before I left, I had an eerie premonition. I cried all the way home.

Ascension Day

I loitered walking home from Mass this morning, savoring this glorious late spring day: bright blue sky, sun shining, flowers blooming, all earth rejoicing in the ascension of our Lord. My heart sings, "This is the day the Lord has made; let us be glad and rejoice in it" (Ps. 118:24).

Forty days have passed since he rose from the dead; the post-Resurrection appearances are over. His human nature now taken into heaven, he exercises all power in heaven and on earth (Matt. 28:18): power to bless, to heal, to sanctify.

The final departure in bodily form of the incarnate God was no matter for sorrow for the disciples, but rather the reverse. They, whose wavering faith had gradually been transformed into a rocklike stability, greeted the ascension of their Lord with joy and worship. Returning to Jerusalem, they "were to be found in the temple, constantly speaking the praises of God" (Luke 24:53). They knew now that he reigned, that the power of darkness and evil had been overcome, that death was only the gateway to life.

We today commemorate his ascension with the same joy as the disciples. We also know that through the ascension we are all kept in close, continuous, personal contact with the risen, glorified Christ, the Lord of our lives, the Lord on whom all life depends. We know now the glorious fulfillment of his promise, "I am with you always, until the end of the world" (Matt. 28:20). And so he is, blessing, forgiving, pouring out upon us the fullness of his healing love.

Sister Virginia came home from the hospital about a week ago. After Mass the following morning, the chaplain had left the oratory carrying the sacrament, preceded as always by the sacring bell, rung by one of the Sisters. I hoped the sacrament was for Sister Virginia, and it was. When the chaplain emerged from her room in the infirmary, I slipped in for a minute to see her. She looks wonderful. It must have been my own fatigue after the mission, and the seven-hour trip home that were responsible for the "premonition" I thought I had felt that night in the hospital.

Pentecost

Ten days ago we celebrated our Lord's Ascension, which was the signal, so to speak, for the coming of the Holy Spirit upon his church, bringing to it knowledge and power and strength, leading us into all truth. The Holy Spirit has come, the third person of the Trinity, God at work in our lives today. And now we are endued with power from on high.

Two thousand years ago the Spirit came upon that group of believers who were to be the church, which is why Pentecost is known as the birthday of the church. All those believers were together in one accord and in one place, as Jesus had instructed them, awaiting the Spirit. And in that coming, the Spirit came also to us, for it is as Peter said, "You must repent and be baptized, each one of you, in the name of Jesus Christ, that your sins may be forgiven; then you will receive the gift of the Holy Spirit. It was to you and to your children that the promise was made, and to all those still far off" (Acts 2:38-39). And this means you and me today and all the generations yet to come.

To be sure, we all received the Holy Spirit at the time of our baptism. For those who are baptized as infants or young children or later, perhaps as mere ritual, appropriation of the Spirit will take the form of conscious, personal commitment to Jesus. Appropriation of the Spirit is never a once-and-for-all experience. As Christians we pray throughout our lives that the Spirit may continually increase in us until we come into God's everlasting kingdom. In response to prayer, there are frequent infillings, so that whatever our task, the Spirit strengthens and empowers us to perform it in Jesus' name.

June 11
St. Barnabas, the Apostle

Barnabas, whose feast we celebrate today, means "son of comfort, the encourager"—surely a fitting name for this apostle and companion of Saint Paul.

"Grant, O God, that we may follow the example of your faithful servant, Barnabas, who, seeking not his own renown but the well-being of your church, gave generously of his life and substance for the relief of the poor and the spread of the gospel" *(Book of Common Prayer)*. This sums up pretty accurately what we attempt to do in and through the healing ministry of the church.

There is a tendency for those who feel they have the gift of healing to chafe under the restraints of the church. Finally, in their impatience, they begin to work alone. When this is done, abuses in the healing ministry occur.

I still remember how appalled I was when, at a mission, a woman stood up during the discussion period and announced that her pastor refused to hold healing services. "*I* believe in the healing ministry," she said, "and so do several of my friends. So *we're* going to start healing services." Involuntarily I exploded, "But you can't do that!" Her response was, "Why not? You do." I most certainly do not. I have always worked under the authority of my church, and know too well that to do otherwise is to court disaster.

I think now of how I have pleaded with those who I believed truly had the gift of healing to be patient and wait. I think with joy and thanksgiving of one friend who has the gift of healing. She waited for fifteen years before she began publicly to exercise this gift. You may say, "Fifteen wasted years because she waited for her church to authorize her work." Not so. The years were not wasted. They were a period of spiritual growth, of steadily increasing knowledge and wisdom. My patient friend could pray, and pray she did. The gifts of the Spirit, of which healing is one, are not the private possession of any single individual. They are given to build up the church, and ultimately they belong *to* the church.

June 28
Irenaeus

Irenaeus, whom we remember today, is known as the first Catholic theologian and is accepted by Catholics and Protestants alike as the church's first systematic theologian. This morning after Mass, I reread portions of his well-known treatise, "Against Heresies." It reminds me that since the beginning of the church there have been heresies to fight. Throughout the New Testament we are cautioned against false doctrine, and with today's turmoil within the church it is vaguely comforting to realize that we are not undergoing anything new. Even the heresies are not new.

I particularly like the emphasis of Irenaeus on Scripture and the traditional elements of the church, insofar as they existed in the early third century. I also like what he says (and for that matter, all the ante-Nicene writers) concerning healing in the church. He speaks at length of driving out demons, the healing of many through the laying-on of hands, and cases of the raising of the dead. "Those who are in truth Christ's disciples," he says, "receiving grace from him, perform miracles. For as [the church] has received freely from God, freely also does she minister to others."

Saints and Angels

July 22
Saint Mary Magdalene

"Almighty God, whose blessed Son restored Mary Magdalene to health of body and of mind, and called her to be a witness of his resurrection: Mercifully grant that by your grace we may be healed from all infirmities and know you in the power of his unending life."

Mary Magdalene—healed by Jesus, his devoted follower, standing by the cross at Calvary. Mary Magdalene—heartbroken, weeping, beside the tomb. Not only have they crucified him, but they have taken away her Lord and she does not know where they have laid him. Mary Magdalene—her grief-stricken face suddenly flooded with rapturous wonder as she hears the beloved voice say, "Mary," and her ecstatic cry, "Rabboni!" (meaning *teacher*), as Jesus in his compassion reveals himself to her. Mary Magdalene—the first witness to the risen Lord and the first messenger of the Resurrection, as she runs to the disciples, exclaiming in breathless excitement, "I have seen the Lord!"

Yesterday a counselee came to me with a problem common to many Christians. She was suffering badly because her father, whom she deeply loves, is dying. He is elderly, and she is a good Christian, so it was not the fact this his death is imminent that primarily distressed her, but rather that he has not accepted Christ. "He's going to die without being saved," my counselee said in real anguish. "What can I do? Where have I failed in bringing him to Jesus? I've been telling my father for years that he must accept our Lord or he will forfeit his salvation."

While it is certainly our holy obligation as Christians to do what we can in and by the power of the Spirit to bring souls to Christ, I must believe on the basis of Scripture that we endure much unnecessary worry over the salvation of our loved ones. We might recall that Jesus did not convert everyone with whom he came in contact. We remember the parable of the seed. The sower is sowing the word. Those on fertile ground listen to the word and take it to heart; those on fallow soil do not. Our Lord never lingered to try to batter people into faith (Mark 4:15-20). He left it to them. "Come unto me," he says, but the "coming" must be voluntary, the free choice of each individual.

Our commission as his followers is to preach the gospel to the world with the knowledge that the entire world will not receive him. What, then, can we do about our beloved unconverted? First, pray as did Saint Monica for her son Augustine. She prayed for many years before her prayers were answered. It behooves us to do the same without discouragement. The one thing we should not do is try to *force* acceptance of Jesus on anyone.

I think that because of our very zeal, we must all be on guard against self-righteousness. To torture ourselves over the lack of salvation of another may possibly be the sin of presumption on our parts. Just perhaps, the inference could be, "I am sure of my own salvation, but surely God can't accept so-and-so." Perhaps it is well for those of us who are committed Christians to concern ourselves with the salvation of our *own* souls, for we are clearly told that "the last shall be first, and the first shall be last" (Matt. 20:16). In the final analysis we are utterly dependent on the mercy and love of God. My final advice yesterday to the suffering daughter was to stop worrying and start praying, and then leave the whole matter in God's all-merciful hands.

September 29
Saint Michael and All Angels

Today is a major feast day, one that (as so many do) seems peculiarly applicable to the healing ministry. The archangel Michael plays an important part in apocryphal literature and is mentioned four times in Scripture. Angels are, in a real sense, colorful threads woven into the fabric of the faith. Primarily they are messengers of God.

The New Testament writers represent Christ as surrounded by angels at the most important times of his life, beginning with the angel announcing to Mary our Lord's conception and subsequent birth. Angels ministered to him in the desert as he underwent his temptations; they strengthened him in his agony at Gethsemane; they met the women who went to the sepulchre.

The Protestant tradition in general has veered away from the subject of angels, and there are reasons for this. However, only lately have I wondered why so many Christians of this day and age and of every branch of the church seem to believe heartily in demons, while rejecting their angelic counterparts. I wonder why we are quicker to speak of Satan and his hordes of demons than to acknowledge the hosts of angels ready to do battle against them and to emerge victorious if we will just call upon them.

After a recent healing service, someone spoke to me of how frightened she was of becoming demon-possessed. I suggested she need not be frightened but just call upon the guardian angel appointed by God to protect her. I think if we were all more aware of the protective power of the angelic host, there would be fewer cases of demon possession. The forces of evil are not stronger than the forces of good. Demons are not stronger than angels, and certainly Satan is not more powerful than God.

Speaking purely personally, I believe in angels because I believe Scripture. Although I have some difficulty with the idea of anything or anyone who seems to come between me and my direct communion with Jesus, I am able to pray with open mind and grateful heart the Saint Michael's Day prayer: "Everlasting God, you have ordained and constituted in a wonderful order the ministries of angels and mortals: Mercifully grant that, as your holy angels always serve and worship you in heaven, so by your appointment they may help and defend us here on earth" (*Book of Common Prayer*).

October 4
Saint Francis of Assisi

This day has very special meaning for me, as it is the one on which I customarily renew my annual vows as a third-order Franciscan. The chaplain received my vows this morning at Mass, and the blessing used so often by Saint Francis, prayed over me, still rings in my ears: "The Lord bless thee and keep thee. May he show his face to thee and have mercy on thee. May he turn his countenance to thee and give thee peace. The Lord bless thee!" And so he has, beyond all my deserts. I was life-professed as a Tertiary years ago, as it seemed the closest I could come to the religious life to which I then felt called.

I have derived much satisfaction in living here in what, for me, is a very Franciscan manner. However, I must admit it is not as Franciscan now as it was when I first came. The community, considering that it fit into the category of "permanent improvement," has put in the most glorious bedroom closet for me, which runs the length of one whole wall. Curious how one's sense of values changes: No longer do I take for granted a large closet. Having been without *any* closet in my bedroom for so long, I now feel I am living in the lap of luxury, and am unashamedly ecstatic!

Actually, I am afraid I am not a very good Franciscan as far as poverty goes. I have one seemingly uncontrollable extravagance: buying books. There is really no excuse for this, as the convent has a large and excellent library. The trouble is, that if I like a book I want to be free to mark and underline passages in it. Obviously this means I must own it. I rationalize this by calling my books the tools with which I work. In a sense this is true, but do I need so *many* tools?

Saint Francis, like the majority of the great saints, was both a contemplative and an activist, a combination of gifts I wish more of us possessed. We tend to be either-or people.

Following the age-long custom of the church, we had the blessing of animals in the chapel this afternoon. Frances, the all-American dog who belongs to one of the Sisters but is in effect the "convent" dog, was first in line. Of course she has lived here a long time, and knows the ropes. In fact, she often comes to the summer services in the chapel, walking through the open door and lying quietly in the sanctuary, sometimes across the feet of the chaplain. On more than one occasion, I have had to step over her to get to the altar rail. As I love dogs, it delights my heart that the Sisters do not even look up when Frances comes to Mass; they take it for granted.

Next in line for her blessing was Jay-Jay, a beautiful dalmatian belonging to another of the Sisters. Then came several cats, followed by various and sundry other animals (including goldfish) brought by the village children. They all behaved with splendid decorum.

"Praised be my Lord by all his creatures." "Let every creature that is in heaven, on earth, and under the earth, and land and sea and all that is in them, praise and exalt him above all forever."

October 23
James of Jerusalem
My train of thought this morning is not to be wondered at, as today we celebrate the feast of Saint James of Jerusalem, who is presumed to be the writer of the Epistle of James. It is on the last chapter of this epistle that the healing ministry of the church is patterned.

"If anyone among you is suffering hardship, he must pray" (James 5:13). The word *hardship* is variously translated as "afflicted" (King James Version), "suffering" (Revised Standard Version), "in trouble" (Jerusalem Bible and Phillips' translation). Regardless of the precise translation, the meaning is clear: Such hardship or affliction is differentiated from physical sickness. The wide scope of the healing ministry is thus unmistakably defined: It embraces all in every area of our lives. The verse immediately following gives specific instruction for the physically ill.

"Is there anyone sick among you? He should ask for the presbyters of the church. They in turn are to pray over him, anointing him with oil in the name of the Lord." This prayer, uttered in faith, will reclaim the one who is ill, and the Lord will restore him to health. If he has committed any sins, forgiveness will be his. "Hence, declare your sins to one another, that you may find healing. The fervent petition of a holy man is powerful indeed" (James 5:14, 16).

The sick, then, are to call for the prayers of the faithful (those who know with their minds and believe in their hearts that Jesus does indeed heal today as he did two thousand years ago). They are to ask for the sacramental healing rite of anointing with oil (holy unction) to be administered by those in the church authorized to do so. The Epistle of James also makes very clear the close correlation between the forgiveness of sin and physical healing.

Our Beloved *Alive*

November 2
All Souls' Day

Yesterday was All Saints' Day, set apart since before the fourth century to celebrate all Christian saints, known and unknown. This morning, at the altar, our beloved dead (or as I think of them, our beloved *alive)* were mentioned by name. However, on this particular All Souls' Day, my heart and mind are filled with but one thing: Sister Virginia. She who never complains has been complaining of severe pains in her back and legs.

At Mass today, she looked extremely well. I chided myself for worrying about her, and reminded myself that one of the worst aspects of cancer is fear of recurrence. Had I fallen into this trap? I believed that she was healed. Why now was I wavering? And yet I found myself wondering if on next All Souls' Day, her name would be on the list of the faithful departed now being read.

The answer was given in the weeks ahead. She was to die, at the age of fifty-eight, a beautiful and holy death. As I watched her die, I thought of how she once said to me, "I read somewhere that frequently, if they pray hard enough, people are granted the boon of dying as they might wish." I am far from sure if this is true, but I know it was so in the case of Sister Virginia.

She had gone into the hospital for tests. On the day I went to visit her, she was just finishing lunch. To my question, "Any news yet from the tests?" she shook her head. At that moment her physician walked in. One look at his face, and I knew why he had come and that the news was bad. As he began to speak, I reached for her hand. The tests had revealed cancer throughout her body. She received the verdict without flinching, but as soon as the doctor left, she said with great anxiety, "All I'm worried about is my father. He's an old man, and this news will kill him." (An aged man to be sure, but one of amazing strength; the painful news did not kill him.) I stayed at the hospital with her for three hours. Neither one of us abandoned hope of her healing here and now, but we faced the possibility that this might not occur.

Sister Virginia received blood transfusions a number of times, but after each transfusion her period of well-being seemed shorter. Two weeks before her death, she went into the hospital for the last time to receive blood. This time she returned not to her own room, but to the infirmary. I was glad of this, for no one is permitted in the Sisters' private wing, but I could visit her in the infirmary.

In her last nine days, she never missed a full day's work as bursar of the community, nor did she miss a single Mass or office with the exception of Compline. She retired early, asking me to visit her each evening after she was in bed. We began most of these evenings by reading Compline together, after which we talked for about an hour. Over these nine days, I watched with something akin to awe, the climax of her lifelong striving for holiness and the perfection to which we all are called as Christians.

She complained of no pain, only that her very keen mind was not as alert as it should be. Each passing day her frustration increased because, as she put it, "What I used to do in ten minutes seems to be taking me longer and longer."

I observed her carefully each day at Mass, as gradually her face took on the unmistakable hue of the terminal cancer patient. At the same time, there was a curious luminosity about her. Though we sat on opposite sides of the oratory, it seemed to me that even with my eyes closed, a brightness shone from her that pierced my eyelids.

On what was to be her last day here, although I did not know it then, she came to Mass as usual but appeared obviously weaker than the day before. I was saddened to think that she should have to miss the Saturday night Prayer and Praise meeting that, to her joy, had recently been inaugurated. Clearly, she would not be well enough tonight to go anywhere, except to bed.

I had been fasting a great deal during the days just passed, and as I had lost considerable weight, decided that I had better eat that night, whether or not I felt like it. To tempt my nonexistent appetite I went to the market and bought two thick lamb chops, a luxury I normally forego because of the price. I had just put them in the broiler when the telephone rang. It was Sister Virginia. "We're waiting for you," she said. "You're late, Emily. Aren't you coming to the Prayer and Praise meeting?"

I gulped, said "Of course," turned off the broiler, and flew. On the way I kept thinking how wonderfully good of God to enable her to go to her beloved meeting.

The large room was filled. Sister Virginia, almost too weak to sit up, was trying to play the guitar. She looked up and smiled as I came in, and another Sister took over the guitar from her. I was grateful and infinitely thankful that so many of the Sisters who ordinarily were not interested in this type of meeting were there tonight. I knew why.

We sang and prayed, and then Sister Virginia said, "My healing is going to be very rapid from now on. Praise the Lord!" Her face seemed to illumine the whole room.

When the meeting was over, two Sisters, one on each side, took her, literally carried her, back to her room. I was walking directly behind them, and she turned back to me and said, "Emily, please come visit me tonight after I'm in bed. Give me about fifteen minutes." Foolishly, I remonstrated, "You're too tired. Let's skip tonight." Thank God she was insistent, so I sat in the foyer of the convent for fifteen minutes and then went back to the infirmary.

She was safely in bed, and rejoicing over the meeting. "You know, Emily, that's the first time Sisters so-and-so ever went. Isn't it great that they were there?" she said delightedly.

Then began what was to be our last talk. For the rest of my life I shall treasure that visit. I cannot reveal what was said, but I shall always be thankful to God that when it was necessary for me to respond, he put words in my mouth. At the end, Jesus himself stood there. "Put your hands in his, Virginia. He will lead you in that unknown way, and it shall be safer for you than any known way." She and I embraced, our tears commingling, and she said, "I can sleep now." I replied, "Yes, you are forever safe in the everlasting arms." And so she was, and is.

As I went out the door she said, "Emily, I'm so glad you're here." Those were the last words I was to hear her speak.

When I was asked to preach the homily at Sister Virginia's Requiem Mass, I was honored, but my first reaction was, "No. I could never get through it." Then I thought for a few minutes and changed my mind, for I realized this would be the last gift I could give my beloved Sister. So I agreed, with deep gratitude for the privilege.

I sat in the choir with the Sisters. Those that passed me, touched my shoulder. I felt their love and prayers as I hope they did mine.

I spoke that day in the power of the Spirit and never was I more thankful.

Thanks be to God for the life of Sister Virginia, for what she meant to so many, and to me.

Thanks be to God for her blithe and joyous spirit, which will always pervade the community she loved so much.

Thanks be to God that she is now completely healed and totally whole in him.

Above all else, thanks be to God who has indeed given us the victory through our Lord Jesus Christ (1 Cor. 15:57).

Expectancy and Celebration

Advent

I love to celebrate whatever the occasion, and seize upon the slightest excuse for festivity! Therefore it pleases me greatly to celebrate three new years: the secular one on January 1, the day my work year starts in September, and above all the church's new year, which began yesterday on the First Sunday of Advent. I think this season of joyful expectancy is my favorite of the church year. From now until December 25 we await the coming of the Lord Jesus, he who has already come yet is still to come. We await him, who though he comes every second of the day—indeed continually indwells us—yet is born anew in our hearts in a different and special way each Christmas Day.

These four weeks before Christmas used to be known as the "Little Lent." In general, this is no longer true, but the keynotes of the season are still and always will be the same: penitence, expectancy, and joy. These could also be termed the keynotes of the healing ministry.

For me, penitence and joy are two sides of the same coin. This is not some personal idiosyncrasy, but the teaching of John the Baptist as I understand it. "Reform your life! [repent]," he cries. "The reign of God [joy] is at hand" (Matt. 3:2).

Penitence, like sin, is an unpopular word; even our churches avoid it as much as possible. Yet penitence during Advent is a far cry from sackcloth and ashes; rather is it the oil of gladness (Heb. 1:9).

Advent is a glorious season indeed, but also a solemn one. Solemn because we seek, insofar as possible, and by God's grace, to become a fit habitation for the King of kings. I think back, now so many years ago, when my husband and I brought home each of our new babies from the hospital, how sparkling clean we made sure the nursery was, how pretty and immaculate the waiting crib. How much more, then, should I seek to have the cradle of my heart pure and beautiful to receive the Holy Child.

The whole season is one of exciting expectancy as we await the rebirth of Jesus in our hearts, as we await his healing touch upon our spirits and our bodies.

Joy is the beginning and the end of Advent. As penitence is simply the other side of the coin of rejoicing without end, so Christian expectancy is not vain hope, but sure and certain knowledge. It is this knowledge possessed by the Christian that gives us joy unspeakable: the knowledge that God loves and cares.

I think of the wonder of the Incarnation, and today it seems to me that one of its greatest joys is my knowledge that "Jesus has been there." I know that wherever I go, I find him waiting for me, strengthening, upholding, empowering by his Spirit. I hear continually in my heart his words: "I will never desert you, nor will I forsake you" (Heb. 13:5). And he never has. "I am with you always, until the end of the world!" (Matt. 28:20). And he is.

December 21
Saint Thomas the Apostle

As we celebrate the feast of Saint Thomas the Apostle, I began the day, as I always seem to on December 21, by feeling confused. Earthbound as I am, it seems curious to celebrate a post-Resurrection event (which is the one most of us associate with Thomas) before our Lord is born! However, in a very real sense, there is deep meaning in this as I invariably come to realize. Thomas, the doubter, the pragmatist, who would not believe until he had probed with his own fingers the nail prints in Christ's hands, and thrust them into his side. He listens to the words, "Do not be faithless, but believing," and Thomas responds with his magnificent confession of faith, "My Lord and my God!"—the first explicit confession of the divinity of Christ. So the words of Thomas are indeed applicable as we prepare ourselves for Christmas, and kneeling before the holy infant cry with Thomas, "My Lord and My God!"

After Mass today I reread with joy a letter received yesterday from a priest in whose church I had recently led a mission. He comments on the strong sense of Christ's presence during those three days; of how denominationalism was swallowed up by the consciousness that we were all, from Roman Catholics to

Pentecostals, simply members of the body of Christ assembled in the presence of our risen Lord and Head. "I felt," he wrote, "as if we had slipped back in time and were with the early apostolic church, sharing its faith and practice. Perhaps, indeed, in a mystery, we were." And then he remarked on the extraordinary love he had experienced for strangers and friends alike throughout the mission.

I think of Paul's words, "He who loves his neighbor has fulfilled the law" (Rom. 13:8), and I remember the man who came to me several months ago for counseling. He had begun by saying, "Well, at least I'm keeping the first and great commandment. I certainly love God with all my heart and soul" (Matt. 22:37). Before I could respond, this good man had launched into a diatribe against his next-door neighbor.

The difficulty is, of course, that the first commandment cannot be separated from the second: to "love your neighbor as yourself." I reflect how it is often much easier to love God whom we have *not* seen, than to love the neighbor of whom we may have seen too much! The way is not easy and Jesus never said it was. "If you love those who love you, what credit is that to you?" he asks. "Even sinners love those who love them" (Luke 6:32).

Jesus prays for those who crucify him; the apostles pray for those who martyr them; the pope prays for his would-be assassin; a couple prays for the killer of their son. All Christians are called to pray for those who persecute them.

I was reminded of this today when I read a letter from the counselee mentioned earlier. He writes that the neighbor whom he thoroughly disliked (and for good *human* reason) suffered a heart attack while mowing his lawn. His family being away, it was my counselee who called the ambulance and rode to the hospital with the stricken man. "Never in my life have I prayed more fervently than for my neighbor on that trip to the hospital." As he prayed, he experienced, in a wonderful way, the love of God which, he said, "filled the ambulance." My friend obviously responded by actually *loving* his neighbor back to life. The neighbor made a good recovery, and my friend says, "I really love that man now. I think he's the closest friend I have."

Jesus says, "This is how all will know you for my disciples: your love for one another" (John 13:35). Every drop of love in one's heart adds to the pool of love in the world, both today and in the ages to come.

On January 31, 1978, I was ordained to the diaconate of the Episcopal Church by Robert B. Appleyard, Bishop of the Episcopal Diocese of Pittsburgh. The ordination took place in Pittsburgh at Trinity Cathedral.

Bishop Appleyard honored me by preaching the ordination sermon. In it he remarked that I had been "spiritually" a deacon for years. This is true in that my calling has been, from the beginning, only to serve. Many have asked me why I wanted to take this step. Among other reasons, it was to express my response to God through the indelible sacrament of ordination: a "yes" to the Lord, forever.

Planning for the ordination was somewhat like planning a wedding. First came the setting of the date. It was no small task to find a time when the bishop was free and when I was between missions. Finally the date was set, and happily it turned out to be the feast day of Saint Marcella, a fourth-century saint of whom I had never heard, but with whom I immediately felt a sense of rapport when I learned that she was noted for her orthodoxy.

The ordination. The great procession of clergy, those priests whom, for so long, I have deeply loved; those who presented me to the bishop on behalf of the clergy and people of the diocese; the much-loved chaplain from the convent, who sang the litany; my beloved friends, the rector from Saint Thomas and one of the women from there who has done so much to further the healing ministry; the priests who came from far distances in terrible weather, including the Roman Catholic priest who drove up from Washington, D.C., over icy roads; the beautiful music; the presence of my children who had come to share it all with me. Finally, as if in a dream, I stood before my bishop for the examination: "My sister, do you believe that you are truly called by God and his church to the life and work of a deacon?" "I believe I am so called." "May the Lord by his grace uphold you in the service he lays upon you." "Amen."

Now, at long last, the ordination prayer. Kneeling before the bishop, his hands upon my head, I hear the prayer as if from far away, "Therefore, Father, through Jesus Christ your Son, give your Holy Spirit to Emily; fill her with grace and power, and make her a deacon in your church." It was the closest to heaven I shall come on this earth.

Epilogue

This collection of the late Reverend Emily Gardiner Neal's writings is offered by the Episcopal Healing Ministry Foundation that "the healing ministry of the Lord Jesus Christ may be taught, proclaimed, and practiced under the authority of the church universal throughout the world." All of Mrs. Neal's writings, published and unpublished, have been given to the Special Collections of Buswell Memorial Library at Wheaton College, Wheaton, Illinois, contributing to a study of outstanding women in the healing ministry.

The Episcopal Healing Ministry Foundation, which is nonprofit and unendowed, is a resource for those seeking a deeper understanding of the healing power of Christ and hoping to begin a healing ministry.

To the Rt. Reverend Herbert Thompson, Jr., Bishop of Southern Ohio, and Lyle Dorsett, Ph.D., of Wheaton College, the Foundation expresses deep gratitude for their assistance in publication of this anthology.

❖ ❖ ❖

Audiocassettes of sermons and written meditations are available from:

Episcopal Healing Ministry Foundation
P.O. Box 206
Terrace Park, OH 45174
(513) 831-8443
www.EpiscopalHealing.org

Topical Index